William

THE MAN WHO WILL BE KING

William

THE MAN WHO WILL BE KING

NICHOLAS DAVIES

BLAKE

Dedication
To Andrea

Published by Blake Publishing Ltd
3 Bramber Court, 2 Bramber Road
London W14 9PB

First published in paperback in Great Britain in 1998

ISBN 1 85782 301 X

British Library Cataloguing-in-Production Data:
A catalogue record for this book is available from the British Library.

Typeset by BCP

Printed and bound in Great Britain by Jarrold Book Printing, Thetford

Pictures reproduced by kind permission of Alpha and Rex Features

Introduction

'Who to Himself is law, no law doth need,
offends no law, is a King indeed...'

George Chapman (1559-1634)

Tall, fair-haired and handsome, Prince William Arthur Philip Louis, the teenager destined to be king, has emerged into public life winning the hearts of countless young women in Britain and around the world and mothers who want to protect and care for him. Never before in England's recent history has an heir to the throne grown up in such a wave of concern and adulation, of genuine acclaim and affection, the world hoping and praying that William and his younger brother Prince Harry will live happier lives than their tragic mother. Following the appalling death of Princess Diana in August 1997 the nation rose up in an extraordinary show of grieving for the young woman who had won the love and admiration of people across the world.

Within days that love and affection had passed from Diana to William and Harry, who, in their youth, seemed so vulnerable and defenceless. The nation demanded that the young princes would be allowed to grow up in peace and privacy, that the paparazzi and the tabloid press would be stopped from hounding them as they had hounded their mother for so many years. And during the year since Diana's death the demands of the nation have been accepted by the paparazzi, the television stations and the tabloids permitting Wills and Harry to carry on their lives without the constant presence of cameras and flash lights.

Overnight almost, Prince William has matured from a shy young boy to a self-assured sixteen year old and teenage girls have taken note. They have become attracted to him in the same way as they would a new young pop star who suddenly emerged on the scene. They appear not to think of William as the heir to the British throne, a young man with the demands of future sovereignty on his mind, but rather as an accessible young man in exactly the same way as their mothers felt that Princess Diana was one of them, a woman apart from royalty who had the same problems as many women. Now, their teenage daughters feel that William is one of them as accessible and approachable as any pop-star or film star might be, someone they can dream about at night and fantasise that one day perhaps they might date.

Prince William is not only good-looking but he also has the easy, warm smile of his mother which devastates people he meets. He is an attractive young man, easy going, with smiling eyes and a certain shyness which people find endearing. He shows no signs of being brash, boastful or bumptious; indeed, he reveals all the traits of being almost the opposite, a friendly, sociable, courteous young man whose character reveals warmth, affection and loyalty.

Suddenly, Prince William has found himself at the centre of 'Willsmania' with lustful teenage girls overcome by passion and emotion wanting to touch him meet him. 'Willsmania' first occurred in Canada in March 1998 when Prince William and Prince Harry, accompanied by their father Prince Charles went on a private family skiing holiday to British Columbia. It was always intended that Charles, flanked by his sons, would undertake a few royal engagements before their holiday on the ski slopes but no one had realised that the presence of young William would have such a devastating affect on the young teenage girls of Vancouver. They came in their scores to see him, they waited patiently to catch a glimpse of him and, when they did, they screamed for him, broke down in tears, fought to touch him and shake his hand, their faces revealing the stress, emotion and raw passion of teenage desire. Never before had a teenage prince of the British royal family been treated in such a fashion. Even during the generations of bygone centuries when it was considered that kings and princes ruled as a divine right was such enthusiasm and passion shown to someone of royal blood.

That royal visit to Canada had a dramatic affect on young William. On all public occasions beforehand, William had shown all the shyness, modesty and nervousness of his mother when she first entered the public arena as Charles's latest girl friend in the late 1970s. Indeed, before the stirring idolatory in Vancouver, William had shown a great antipithy towards appearing in public, shying away from chaos, scrutiny and grind that often comes with public duties. Previously, William had usually coped with public appearances by putting his head down, staring at the ground in front of him and walking briskly towards his destination, not wanting to be seen by the cheering admirers, not wanting to give an opportunity to the cameramen to get a shot of his face. And it had worked.

He adopted this technique of non-co-operation on his arrival in Canada. But then, in the Waterfront Centre Hotel in Vancouver where the royal party was staying, Charles had a chat with his son, bolstered his confidence and urged him to go out the following day and chat to those who had been waiting hours for a glimpse of their new star. He advised him to act naturally, chat to a few of those who were calling for his attention, shake a few hands, make a couple of light-hearted remarks and smile to everyone.

Blushing a little at first, and appearing somewhat diffident, the shy prince walked out of the hotel to a crescendo of screams and acclamation. Blushing openly he walked over to the lines of teenage girls who were waiting to see him and began shaking some by the hand, while, at the same accept gifts of beloved teddy bears which the girls gave him as heartfelt presents, openly declaring their love and admiration. He responded as naturally as his mother responded to crowds of wellwishers and supporters; he smiled like a Hollywood actor, he answered their questions, shook their hands and took their gifts, thanking all of them. In turn, they responded by declaring undying love for him.

The result was captured by television crews and photographers who had also waited patiently for a few shots of the handsome prince who seemed to have won the hearts of Vancouver's younger set. The pictures were flashed around the world, the television networks broadcast the shots on main news items, newspapers and magazines devoted pages of pictures and comment to the new sensational phenomenom who no one had noticed had grown from a somewhat shy, gauche young kid into a strapping, handsome and most attractive young man. And he was only fifteen.

Opposite page: Vancouver, Canada 1998. Willsmania takes hold.

Chapter One

'Lead an adventurous and honourable youth'

Robert Louis Stevenson (1850-1894)

As dusk was falling at the end of a bright summer's day on June 21, 1982, the future King of England, William Arthur Philip Louis, gulped his first breath of air. The little lad weighed 7lb 10oz and had a wisp of fair, blondish hair, and clear blue eyes. Doctors pronounced the heir to the throne fit and healthy and William proved it by yelling lustily as his exhausted mother started to breast feed him. His father, the Prince of Wales, who had been at his wife's side throughout the 16-hour-long labour, was euphoric, phoning his parents, brothers and sisters with the good news. After all, his wife, Diana, had just ensured that the blood line of the House of Windsor was safe for at least another generation. Only 36 hours after the end of a long and difficult labour, Princess Diana checked herself out of the private wing of St Mary's hospital in Paddington, London, and into the noise of the waiting crowds, photographers and TV crews. Wrapped in a lace shawl and carried in the proud arms of his father, the as yet unnamed heir to the throne slept through the mayhem of his first photocall. As the rest of the country celebrated, the exhausted Princess watched proudly as her husband carried her tiny son into a limousine and held him in his arms as they made their way back to Kensington Palace and the beginning of William's life as a vital part of the most famous family in the world.

It took seven days of discussion and argument before the name of the new heir was officially announced, leading to furious speculation in the newspapers and frenzied betting at bookmakers. It was known that Diana favoured Sloaney names such as Sebastian and Oliver, whilst Charles had been holding out for Albert after Queen Victoria's consort. In the end, compromise won the day, with William being seen as a comfortable mixture of the traditional and the trendy.

From the moment Diana realised she was pregnant, both parents were determined to enjoy her pregnancy. Prince Charles read numerous books on the role of fathers during labour and even attended a lecture on childbirth, whilst the Princess of Wales herself was wearing maternity dresses and coats long before her size made it necessary. In all, it was a very public pregnancy, with photographers allowed unprecedented access to the Princess of Wales. In fact, it was probably one of the most talked about pregnancies in history, with commentators rushing to explain the historical significance of the royal birth, health writers endlessly pronouncing on the various stages of pregnancy and everyone else speculating on the sex of the unborn child. The princess always maintained in public that she had no idea whether her first born would be male or

Opposite page: Princess Diana with baby William.

female. In private however, a scan during the later stages had left her and Charles in no doubt that she was expecting a boy. From the start, Diana was determined to break with all the royal traditions that had been explained to her. Her demand to give birth in a hospital was one which left the royal advisers in a spin. Previously, all royal babies, and especially those born to be heir to the throne, had been born in Buckingham Palace surrounded by nurses, midwives and doctors in a room equipped as a labour ward. But Diana was determined that if anything should go wrong with the birth, her baby would have immediate access to all the latest neo-natal technology. Charles, too, was brought round to her point of view and so William came into the world in a public hospital.

The princess always maintained in public that she had no idea whether her first born would be male or female.

Charles however, was not so convinced when it came to the choice of nannies for his first-born. Like most upper-class children, he had been cared for by a nanny from an early age, and for William, he wanted his old nanny, Mabel Anderson, who was well versed in royal protocol. But Diana had other ideas. She didn't want an old-fashioned regulated routine for her son. She wanted a nanny who was informal and progressive and who, more importantly, would play second fiddle to her in the nursery. Secretly, Diana did not want anyone to look after her beloved baby; she wanted to do it all herself, but she accepted that she needed help. She was the Princess of Wales and it was her duty to accompany her husband to many official functions. What she couldn't and wouldn't accept was that she might be superseded in her own child's affection by a hired help. In the end, Charles swallowed his objections and agreed to the appointment of Barbara Barnes, the 42-year-old daughter of a forestry worker, a no-nonsense lady who had no formal training, never wore a uniform and, most importantly, did not regard the royal nursery as her own private kingdom or herself as a mother substitute. Barbara was not alone in the nursery for she also had a helper,

The sailor Prince at a wedding, July 1986.

Olga Powell, an experienced nursery maid. The system worked well. Charles and Diana wandered in and out of the nursery at will. The Prince took great delight in changing nappies and bathing his tiny son, and Diana spent hours talking and playing with her little boy. When William displayed any symptoms of childish illnesses such as a snuffle or a cough, it was Diana who slept beside his cot in the night nursery.

If Diana won the battle of the nannies, it was most definitely her husband who was responsible for choosing the godparents. Diana had wanted at least one of her young friends from her pre-wedding days to be included in the list. Instead, the nearest person to her age was Tally, wife of the richest landowner in England, the Duke of Westminster. And Tally was asked to be a godparent because her husband and Prince Charles were good friends. Otherwise, the list included the former King Constantine of Greece, a close friend of Charles; Lady Susan Hussey, one of the Queen's senior Ladies-in-Waiting; Princess Alexandra; and Lord Mountbatten's grandson, Lord Romsey. The choice which raised the most eyebrows was that of the now deceased Sir Laurens van der Post who was seventy-six at the time, and a close friend of Charles. Sir Laurens, Japanese POW survivor, philosopher, poet and storyteller was seen as a wildcard entry. On the afternoon of August 4, 1982, surrounded by his godparents in the music room at Buckingham Palace, Prince William was christened. One by one, the godparents pledged to bring him up in the Christian faith, and to help and guide him throughout his life. As time would show, William was to need all the help he could get in the traumatic years ahead.

When William displayed any symptoms of childish illnesses such as a snuffle or a cough, it was Diana who slept beside his cot in the night nursery.

Both Charles and Diana were determined that William should have a happy and normal childhood, and crucial to this was the decision that the parents would not spend long periods of time away from him. When Charles was a baby he would only see his mother twice a day, once for thirty minutes around nine o'clock and then, for a further thirty minutes in the early evening. At all other times, nannies cared for Charles for the first five years of his life. Charles also remembered the desolation he felt when his own mother, the Queen, put duty before children and disappeared from their lives for months at a time visiting various parts of the Commonwealth. The world witnessed one reunion after the Queen had been away on a royal tour for six long months, when mother and son treated each other politely, like strangers. On that occasion, Charles was told to greet his mother with a handshake. And that's what happened. There were no kisses or hugs, no laughter and no playfulness. Charles had often told Diana of his misery at feeling that his mother was far away from him – Diana was having none of it for her child. So when it was time to go to Balmoral for the annual royal summer holiday, the three of them flew together and it was Charles who carried his son off the plane while the nanny walked behind carrying the baby equipment.

Opposite page: William and Prince Diana at polo.

Six months later, in January 1983, Charles decided that Diana needed a holiday away from her son. Exhausted from trying to combine the duties of being the wife to the

Prince of Wales, and all that entailed, with constantly caring for William, Diana's health was causing concern. But the break, a week in Liechtenstein at the castle of Prince Franz Joseph, was not a happy one. Diana spent much of the time in tears, missing William and – some believed – it seemed she was suffering from post-natal depression. The couple came back to England in the worst of spirits with Diana, especially, determined that she would never be parted from William again, without good reason.

Her resolve was soon put to the test. A royal tour of Australia for the couple had been announced shortly after William was born, which would take them away from Britain for six weeks. Diana made her feelings clear; she was not going to be separated from Prince William at such a crucial stage in his development. The arguments raged between Kensington and Buckingham Palace, with the Queen eventually interceding and agreeing that Charles and Diana could take the young Prince with them. Thus, in the spring of 1983, the young family arrived in Australia, complete with Nanny Barnes and a whole host of baby equipment, organic foods, vitamins and food supplements. With his nanny, William was settled in the tiny town of Woomargama in New South Wales, whilst his mother and father criss-crossed the country, meeting almost a million people. Whenever they could, they flew back to spend time with their son. It was another successful break with protocol and, although other trips were made without William, it set the pattern for Diana within the royal family. William came first, no matter what royal protocol dictated.

Like his father before him, William was a precocious little child. Surrounded by his doting nanny, talked to and played with by his parents, he had an early vocabulary and was naturally curious. During the 1983 summer holiday in Balmoral, when just fifteen months old, William was left to his own devices for just a few minutes and spotted a tempting button on the nursery wall. He pushed it, sending an alarm signal to the Aberdeen police headquarters. It wasn't until the police had raced to Balmoral, sealed off the castle and the entire grounds, that it was discovered that William had been responsible for the furore. Barbara Barnes was beside herself with embarrassment, while Prince Charles and Diana thought it was all a bit of a hoot.

... his behaviour was beginning to ring alarm bells with the Queen and Prince Philip.

Like most toddlers, William was into everything. His favourites trick was flushing anything he could get his hands on down the loo, including his father's shoes. Like millions of parents before them, Diana and Charles found all this childlike mischief hilariously endearing and, instead of chastising the little boy, they nicknamed him Wombat (an Australian small bear). For the time being at least, Prince William was unconditionally adored, unbelievably pampered and the centre of his parent's world.

But in January 1984, Princess Diana discovered she was pregnant for the second time, and on September 15, 1984, when Prince William was just twenty months old, she gave birth to a second son, Prince Henry Charles Albert David, to be known as Harry. And, once again, Diana was admitted to St Mary's Hospital. Fears that William may have felt some jealously towards his younger brother had worried Diana throughout her second pregnancy. She had consulted her friends, who also had young families, about the subject and read up on it wherever she could find information. Although she was determined to leave the hospital soon after Harry's birth, she insisted that William must visit them first to establish a bond with the new baby as soon as possible. The morning after the birth, William, Prince Charles and Nanny Barnes were driven to St Mary's and brought up to see the new arrival. Diana heard her son coming as soon as he stepped out of the lift. Diana was waiting and scooped him into her arms so that she was holding him when he first saw his baby brother.

Any fears that she may have had about William harbouring jealous feelings towards his younger brother were quickly dispelled. In fact, it was an early indication of his caring nature that he took to the little baby in a big way. From the first moment that he saw Harry he was enthralled, he wanted to hold him and play with him at every opportunity. In fact, when Harry was christened three months later in St Geroge's chapel in the grounds of Windsor Castle, William – or Wills, as he was often called – made a bit of a nuisance of himself when he was told he couldn't hold his little brother. In front of millions of TV viewers, William ran unchecked through the distinguished gathering, even ignoring the Queen as she attempted to reason with her little grandson. There was no doubt that William was becoming what was euphemistically termed 'a bit of a handful' and his behaviour was beginning to ring alarm bells with the Queen and Prince Philip as well as the disciplined Prince Charles. He had an uphill struggle ahead of him. Diana, who had worked with children before she married, was completely relaxed with William, thinking nothing of bribing him into good behaviour or laughing at his antics when perhaps she should have been disapproving. Nanny Barnes, too, doted on her young charge and was often reluctant to administer the discipline that all young children need. The signs that something was wrong were clear. Shortly after Harry's christening, the Queen Mother invited the family to Birkhall, her Scottish residence, and Prince William ran riot, apparently almost destroying her dining room. He also earned himself a bad reputation with some of the servants, showing disrespect and being rude to them in ways which infuriated his father.

Finally, Diana agreed that Wills was getting out of hand and that something had to be done. She accepted that it was time to stop pampering William's every whim and begin the transition from babyhood to childhood. Wills was three. Charles was all for William following the royal tradition of having his early education at home with a governess teaching him the rudiments of reading and writing. But Diana felt that her son would benefit more from mixing with other children, and having playmates of his own age. One afternoon, as she was visiting potential kindergarten's with William, she watched as he tried to join in with the other children. Within a few minutes, it became clear that although William desperately wanted to join in the fun and games, he couldn't – because he didn't know how. That night she told Charles about the sad little incident and he finally agreed that William should go to a kindergarten. As with everything to do with their beloved son, Charles and Diana thought long and hard about their choice of school for him. Diana, in particular, was in her element, researching, asking friends and relatives and visiting several places, before finally settling on Mrs Minors' school in Notting Hill Gate, a few minutes' drive from Kensington Palace.

William with Prince Charles at Aberdeen airport, September 1984.

Charles recalled the fuss that had attended his first day at school and he desperately wanted to spare William that ordeal. So, together, he and Diana sat down and composed a letter to all the national newspaper editors, asking them to leave William to attend school in peace. Mrs Minors spoke to neighbours in the quiet leafy street, while Diana personally spoke to the parents of every child at the school, in an attempt to prevent leaks to the press and to apologise beforehand for any inconvenience William's attendance might cause. Other precautions were also necessary. Some of the windows in the building had to be replaced with bullet-proof glass, an alarm and panic button had to be installed in William's classroom and provision had to be made for the armed detective who would be with William at all times.

'When I'm King, I'm going to send all my knights round to kill you.'

On a sunny September day in 1985, William arrived for his first day at school wearing a pair of red shorts and a checked shirt. He hardly blinked at the phalanx of 150 photographers and TV cameramen who had lined up to record the day. In fact, it was his mother Diana who seemed to be the more nervous of the two. It was a friendly, happy school, with three classes of twelve pupils. William started in the Cygnets class, moved on to the Little Swans and finally progressed to the Big Swans. In this cosy environment he enjoyed all the games and fun common to most pre-schoolers – finger painting, water play and modelling, as well as learning to count and being introduced to the rudiments of reading and writing. But if Diana and Charles had hoped that the young Prince would have some of his less attractive qualities quickly rubbed off him by his schoolmates, they were to be disappointed. A bright little boy, William quickly learned how to pull rank on the other children.

'If you don't do what I want I'll have you arrested,' was one phrase which could be often heard echoing around the playground. His assigned bodyguard often had to calm down his young charge, but sometimes Wills was too quick for him and a fight would have started in the time it took for the bodyguard to look away. Within weeks, William had been nicknamed 'Basher'.

On another occasion, Wills pushed even his doting mother too far. One of the children at the kindergarten was having a birthday party and Wills was playing up badly. He refused to sit down quietly with the other children, and when he was told off he threw his food on the floor. When he was ordered to pick up the mess, he shouted at the staff, 'When I'm King, I'm going to send all my knights around to kill you.' When Diana was told of his behaviour at the end of the party, she was extremely embarrassed and not a little angry at her son's high-handed behaviour. She told him that if he did such a thing again, he would be punished. But William's unruly behaviour came as no surprise to Diana. At home, Wills had by now become quite a handful, demanding and getting his own way, being rude and cheeky to everyone, and refusing to do what either his mother or Nanny Barnes told him to do. He would refuse to go to bed at night, demand that people fetch and carry his toys for him and, on many occasions, Diana would placate her first-born by finding and bringing the toys to him. He would also refuse to put away his toys when asked, which resulted in many stand-offs between Wills and his mother. Generally speaking, however, the little lad would obey his father, but only after a minute or so of argument. In principle, both

Opposite page: William at polo, 1989.

Diana and Charles were against smacking their children but, on occasions, William was given a hard slap on the behind if they thought he had gone too far. On one occasion, while watching his father play polo at Windsor Great Park, William went up to a little girl and pushed her to the ground. His mother witnessed the incident, grabbed hold of William and gave him a good hard whack on the backside. Wills looked at his mother in some astonishment and anger. But he did do as he was told and apologised to the little girl.

William was a disaster. He fidgeted throughout the vows, stuck his tongue out at the young bridesmaids and generally behaved like a naughty little boy.

But those times of discipline were few and far between. In reality, both Diana and Nanny Barnes were far too soft with him. Prince Charles, with his strong sense of duty and protocol, and memories of his disciplined upbringing, had begun to worry that his son was running wild and would begin to attract criticism. Even in public, Wills had begun to show signs of being unruly. Charles was especially upset by his son's behaviour at the wedding of Sarah Ferguson to Prince Andrew in 1986. Prince William was a page boy, but whilst the other children were models of good behaviour throughout the ceremony, William was a disaster. He fidgeted throughout the vows, stuck his tongue out at the young bridesmaids and generally behaved like a naughty little boy. This time, the TV cameras captured his antics and Charles was extremely upset. He continued to try, in the face of some opposition from Diana, to instill a sense of discipline into his little boy, to be consistent in his parenting. But the Prince was often away on royal duties and it became obvious that the liberal Nanny Barnes would have to be replaced by someone who would take a stronger line with both William and his younger brother Harry.

At that time, Prince William was ready to move up to his pre-prep school, Wetherby, just five minutes from Kensington Palace, and it was decided that Barbara Barnes would take the opportunity to leave. There were, in fact, two reasons for asking Barbara Barnes to leave. One was that Diana had become somewhat jealous of the relationship between Nanny Barnes and William, who seemed to adore her. And Prince Charles believed that Barbara Barnes was too easy going. Charles believed his son, then aged five, needed some discipline and, in January 1987, Barbara Barnes left royal employment to continue her career. Her replacement was Ruth Wallace, a brisk and businesslike woman who had worked with sick children before becoming nanny to the family of the ex-King Constantine of Greece, a close friend of Prince Charles. Within weeks, a change was noticed in the behaviour of the two boys as 'Nanny Roof', as they called her, began to weave her magic. She encouraged them to be friendly to all the servants at Kensington Palace and Highgrove, to play by themselves nicely and, most importantly, instilled in them a sense of routine and discipline. An important concession was made by Diana. She agreed, after much lobbying by the Prince of Wales, that if Nanny Wallace felt it was deserved, she would be allowed to smack Prince William. But despite her best intentions, Diana still managed to sabotage Nanny Wallace from time to time, often comforting William if he had been punished for being naughty.

A typical day for William began at 7.30am, when Ruth would wake him and his brother, wash them, dress them and give them their breakfast at the nursery table. Although their parents were often busy getting ready for public duties, the boys would always see them before each went their separate ways, the boys to school, the parents to work. William in particular would salute his father with a giggle when he said goodbye to him. Whenever she could, Diana would drive them to school herself, and always tried to be back at Kensington Palace to read bedtime stories and kiss them goodnight. On Friday afternoons, like many upper-class London families, the Waleses would drive out of town to stay at their country home, Highgrove House, in Gloucestershire for the weekend. There, the boys began to love and appreciate the countryside, visiting the farm which was attached to the estate, playing in the trees and riding their little ponies. William, in particular, used to push his new-found freedom to the limit, often disappearing just around bedtime so that he could gain a few precious extra moments of playtime. But by and large, his behaviour was improving. Having quickly settled into his new school, with its heavy emphasis on manners, William soon learned how to behave in respectable company. He perfected the art of opening doors for women and calling men 'Sir'. He could shake hands like a man and even had his own form of royal wave. Prince Charles and Princess Diana heaved a sigh of relief. At last, their royal heir was beginning to act like one.

Perhaps it was hardly surprising that Prince William was behaving in a rebellious manner. As any armchair psychologist would say, young children who behave badly are often expressing what they cannot say vocally, that all is not well with their world. And all was certainly not well between William's parents. By the end of 1985, his parents' marriage, which had started with such love and mutual admiration, had developed gaping cracks. Diana's eating problems, her bulimia and neuroses, combined with Charles' return to his old love, Camilla Parker Bowles, had meant the royal couple were living all but separate lives. And when they were together, the world could see that the atmosphere between them was tense and cold. By 1987, Charles was spending most of his time at Highgrove House. He moved all his personal affects out of Kensington Palace and then moved his official office to Highgrove, hardly ever spending a night in London. Diana was left to stay alone in London, enjoying her life with Wills and Harry. Despite her upbringing, Diana didn't like life in the country, preferring the sophistication, the restaurants, the shops and the buzz of London life. As a result, Wills and Harry only saw their father when they travelled to Highgrove for weekends. And even those precious few days were often grim affairs, with meals being taken in near silence and little of the sense of the fun and games that had characterised their visits in earlier years. The relationship between Diana and Charles had reached rock bottom and they found it difficult to be courteous to each other, let alone have a reasonable, amicable conversation. As a result, during those weekends, Charles would spend the days in the walled garden while Diana, with the help of detectives and household staff, entertained and amused the boys. Charles tried to involve William in gardening, and to that end he bought him a miniature set of garden tools so he could join in, but Wills showed little inclination for the idea. It wasn't long before Charles lost his patience and the scheme ended in tears.

> William, in particular, used to push his new found freedom to the limit.

Perhaps to compensate for the stuffiness of their father, or perhaps to spite him, Princess Diana began to take the boys on outings to theme parks such as Alton Towers, go-cart racing or even to burger bars. She took William to the theatre to see *Joseph and the Amazing Technicolour Dreamcoat* and to Wimbledon to watch the All-England finals from the superb vantage point of the Royal Box. William loved sport of any kind and preferably at the highest speed. He was an adept horseman from an early age, vaulting on and off his bareback pony with ease and even riding his sturdy Shetland pony while standing on the saddle! At Wetherby school, William excelled in running and the high jump. At Ludgrove, he was somewhat hesitant on the football field, but with encouragement he became a good, even aggressive, football, and was selected to play for the school's first team. His sports master wrote that William showed bravery and precision on the ball. Like his mother, he was also a natural at tennis, and he was taught to swim at an early age. He used to love accompanying his mother to the swimming pool at Buckingham Palace, as well as the other pools she frequented in health clubs in London. As Diana commented, 'sometimes William is more like a fish the way he swims and dives, a natural.' But to the delight of his father, William also showed that he loved traditional country sports as much as he enjoyed the thrill and speed of go-carting and skateboarding. From the age of four, when he was taken to watch his first game shoot on the Sandringham Estate, he was hooked. At that first shoot he brandished his toy gun at the sky, at seven he was learning to 'beat' – to drive the pheasants towards the shoot – and by ten he had learned the rudiments of how to be a good shot.

Learning to ride with Maureen Cox, the Highgrove groom, April 1988.

William was becoming something of a rebel as well as a dare-devil, earning a reputation for often getting into scrapes, running into trees, fences, iron bars and lumps of concrete. He also loved climbing trees, the taller the better. On occasions, his detective had to rescue him, guiding him down from trees fifty feet high. He was renowned for constantly hurting himself, though after a few tears he would return to whatever game he had been playing, taking the risks once again. Ever since he was four, William's favourite games involved brandishing his arsenal of plastic toy guns, rifles, pistols and swords. He was an ace with water pistols, with a reputation for aiming with unerring accuracy at people, much to their consternation. He also loved teasing women, especially his mother. When he was five years-old, he developed a naughty habit of pinching her bottom, making her jump. Usually, Diana screamed with laughter, encouraging her young son. But then William began pinching other womens' bottoms, including maids and servants and friends who came to visit Diana at Kensington Palace. Once, he was caught pinching a woman's bottom at a school sports day and Diana had to

put her foot down. He was becoming a little menace. Staff at Highgrove have never forgotten the day when five-year-old William dug up a buried rabbit from the compost heap, swinging it around his head and yelling for his mother to look. He threatened to throw it at her but Diana's screams deterred him and he put the carcass back on the compost heap.

In 1990, William's time as a day boy, going to school each morning and coming home every afternoon, was over. Much to Diana's distress, it was time for the little boy to be sent away from home, to become a boarder. But Diana herself had been sent to boarding school as a young girl and she believed that boarding would help William settle down, direct his energies, and encourage him to understand his responsibilities. Yet again, a great deal of thought and research went into the choice of schools. The home counties of England are renowned for top-quality prep schools, many specialising in different areas of excellence. After

William was something of a rebel as well as a daredevil

much research, Diana and Charles settled on Ludgrove Preparatory School in Berkshire. Handy for the road network, reasonably close to both his mother in London and his father in Gloucestershire, the school had a friendly, homely atmosphere with a good record in sport. Most importantly, it was hidden from prying eyes, set in 130 acres, well back from public roads and almost impossible to spy upon. On the first day of the September term 1990, Prince William, along with his mother and father mounted the steps of the £2,100 per term school and shook hands with the headmaster Gerald Barber. On saying their goodbyes, Diana dissolved into tears while William remained gravely composed. The transition from boy to man had begun.

In truth, his departure to school was probably a blessing in disguise, for by the winter of 1990, his parents were engaged in a cold war of such ferocity that those around them were left in no doubt as to their mutual hatred. Just about managing to hold their emotions in check for public engagements, often the couple would drive away in the same car, only to split up as soon as they were out of sight and go their separate ways. The media were, of course, in full flow, speculating endlessly about the true nature of the Royal relationship, and while palace officials tried desperately to paper over the cracks, to seasoned observers there was no doubt that this was a marriage in deep trouble. As in all troubled marriages, it was almost impossible for the children to be kept out of the arguments and this one was no different. On occasions, William had been witness to some of the screaming matches which occurred whenever the Royal couple did manage to get together, usually at Highgrove. After one particularly nasty row, while his mother was sobbing in a locked bathroom, William pushed some tissues under the door with a note saying, 'don't cry Mummy'. After another row, he telephoned her favourite restaurant, San Lorenzo, in Beauchamp Place, London, and booked a table for the two of them, to cheer her up.

But despite being away at school, the pressure of his parents' unhappiness was weighing heavily on him. Other boarders reported to their parents that he would often wander around the grounds on his own, shoulders hunched and hands in pockets, looking as if the cares of the world were on his shoulders. Even the care that the teachers took to shield William from the news and gossip that was floating around was irrelevant. William knew that his parents couldn't stand the sight of each other. And that made him very unhappy. One incident must have served as a bleak reminder to William just how far apart his parents were. On June 3, 1991, he was playing golf with friends at the school when one of them accidentally hit him a crashing blow to the head with an iron club. William collapsed, knocked unconscious with blood pouring from the wound. By the time he reached the casualty department of the Royal Berkshire Hospital, a distraught Diana and Charles were by his side. As doctors examined the wound and pronounced it to be serious, his parents began arguing about the best place to send their son. Charles wanted him to go to the Queen's Medical Centre in Nottingham where he had been treated for a broken arm the previous year, while Diana, accepting the advice of the senior doctor present, insisted that he go to Gt Ormond Street Hospital for Sick Children. Diana's will prevailed and she sat in the ambulance with William as it raced towards London, accompanied by police cars and motorcycle outriders. A defeated and chastised Charles followed behind in his Aston Martin sports car. At the London hospital, physicians explained that William had suffered

He would often wander around the grounds on his own, shoulders hunched and hands in pockets, looking as if the cares of the world were on his shoulders.

a depressed fracture of the skull and needed an operation to ascertain the damage. While Diana sat with her son as he came round from the seventy-five minute operation and stayed with him through that long night, Prince Charles had to continue with his royal duties, and sat through a performance of the opera Tosca at Covent Garden. After phoning the hospital to check on William's condition, Charles then boarded a night train to York where he was to discuss green issues with various organisations.

Despite his troubles, William was beginning to blossom into a young teenager. His manners were impeccable and he had become far more thoughtful to other people. On one of the royal family's visits to Crathie church, near Balmoral, he spontaneously turned to his great grandmother, the Queen Mother, and assisted her down the aisle of the church and out through the gateway to her waiting car. He then turned to his mother and escorted her to her car. In addition, the golden boy was displaying all the signs of turning into a top-class athlete. Academically, despite some press reports to the contrary, William was showing his mettle, in the top third of his class at Ludgrove and always the first to put his hand up for parts in the school plays. He was also becoming closer to his mother, ringing her almost every night from school and writing regular updates about his day-to-day life at the school. William had become concerned for his mother's happiness, and he saw his role as a protector, making sure she remained happy. She would sometimes drive up from London to pay him visits, and the two of them would wander off into the grounds laughing and joking with a closeness that Prince Charles could only envy.

To many, it seemed as if William had become the one person his mother could rely on for unconditional love.

To many, it seemed as if William had become the one person his mother could rely on for unconditional love and many observers began to worry that she was placing too much pressure on her young son. She called him 'the man in my life' and in picture after picture of the two of them are seen together, Diana almost physically leaning on young William for support. She probably felt she needed all his love and his strength, for in 1992, the crisis of the royal marriage was brought dramatically into the open, with books detailing Diana's misery. Aggravating the situation further, tapes of a conversation between Diana and her friend James Gilbey were published, revealing Diana's bitterness towards the Royal Family, whom she believed were deliberately pushing her aside. The tapes also revealed how Diana wanted to be free of them, and free of her husband. Within a few short weeks, all the pretence had been stripped away and the truth of the sham that was the royal marriage was there for the world to see. Throughout the autumn of 1992, as Prince Charles, Princess Diana and the Queen sought to make sense of the highly embarrassing mess, Prince William was left at Ludgrove, and had to cope with the frenzy of press speculation which faced him whenever he happened to see a newspaper. Doubtless there were the comments and jokes of his school mates to contend with, too, and all in all, it was a pretty miserable time for the ten-year-old boy.

By December 1992, the Palace had admitted defeat – a reconciliation between the couple was totally out of the question, the royal fairytale was well and truly over. On December 9, Prime Minister John Major rose to his feet in the House of Commons to read out the statement that the Prince and Princess of Wales would be separating after eleven years of marriage. The day before, a tearful Diana had driven up to Ludgrove to tell her son of the decision, and to talk through its implications. To his eternal credit, the young William responded to this dreadful news with a maturity far beyond his years. He turned to his mother, kissed her on the cheek and said, 'I hope you will both be happier now'.

Chapter Two

'He wears the rose of youth upon him'

Shakespeare, *Anthony and Cleopatra* Act 11

On December 9, 1992, Prime Minister John Major made a statement to a hushed House of Commons, announcing that the Prince and Princess of Wales were to separate after eleven years of marriage. The only surprise to Members of Parliament, who had crowded into the Commons for the statement, was the Prime Minister's remark that the separation would have 'no constitutional implications' and that Diana could still be crowned Queen. As expected, Mr Major's statement said the the couple's decision to lead separate lives had been reached amicably, that both would continue to carry out public duties, and that both would participate fully in the upbringing of the two young princes. To William, then ten, and Harry, then eight, enjoying the end of term plays and carol service, the news did not come as a shock but, nevertheless, William was unhappy that his parents were to live apart. In truth, he felt somewhat humiliated that his parents needed to separate officially and announce the fact to the world. William naturally found the whole process deeply upsetting and, as a result, during that final week at school before the Christmas holidays, he became somewhat introvert, not wanting to mix with the other boys, preferring to keep out of the limelight, fearing he might be teased about his parents divorce. Of course, the teachers tried to encourage him, to bring back his self-confidence, but William remained somewhat subdued and quiet. William felt, different, awkward. No other boys amongst all his friends had to put up with the embarrassment of having their parents' private lives splashed over the newspapers all the time. In fact, neither William nor Harry hardly ever saw any newspapers at school – and certainly not the sensational tabloids – because all tabloids were banned at Ludgrove in a bid to prevent the two young princes seeing what was written about their parents. Nevertheless, of course, on occasion the boys did come across tabloid newspapers and, invariably, there would be a salacious, and often inaccurate, story about his parents on the front page. William would confess later that whenever he saw a tabloid with a picture of either his mother or father on the front page, he would have a sinking feeling in the pit of his stomach for fear of what was being written about them. It was this gnawing antipathy, built up over a number of years, that was partly responsible for William's hatred of all newspapers, and particularly the tabloids.

The separation changed nothing, however, for either William or Harry. As before, they continued to visit their father at Highgrove and, for two weeks of the holiday, stayed with their mother at Kensington Palace. But Christmas they spent at Sandringham with their father and the rest of the Royal family. William, however,

Opposite page: Strawberries and cream for William, June 1987.

found Christmas an awkward time, except for the days he spent with his father, and sometimes other members of the family, out in the fields, or riding. Sandringham and Balmoral always seemed claustrophobic to him, because he felt he always had to be on his best behaviour in the presence of the Queen and Prince Philip. He noted how his father was always totally respectful towards his mother and knew that he, too, had to behave in the same way and he found that rather tedious. Outside, however, he could relax and enjoy himself, not having to watch how he used his knife and fork; not having to wait to be spoken to before making any remark; not having to dress correctly for meals; not having to remember how he should address maids, footmen, valets and cooks, as well as all the important guests, such as politicians and their wives, who sometimes came to stay.

Even when William knew he was being cheeky or naughty, his mother would usually roar with laughter

It wasn't that the Queen and Prince Philip didn't show kindness, chat to him in a friendly manner, or try to make him feel 'at home' at Sandringham or Balmoral. His grandparents did all these things and they would usually smile and be friendly whenever they met, whether at table, the drawing room or walking around the buildings. And yet always William found himself on the defensive whenever he met them. He wasn't totally sure how he should approach them because he noted that everyone else treated them with deep respect and courteous civility at all times, the servants standing to attention and bowing their heads whenever they met the Queen walking along a corridor. It was all so different from life at Kensington Palace, Highgrove or even at school.

For William, life at Kensington Palace, with Harry and his mother, was so often full of laughter and fun. William loved to run into his mother's bedroom in the morning, give her a cuddle in bed and play with toys, with all of them laughing and shouting at the same time. He used to enjoy the pillow fights with his mother screaming in mock horror whenever he managed to hit her in the face with a pillow or when Harry would join his mother in the fight against him. Meals were also fun, with no stuffy manners, having to check when it was acceptable to start in case the Queen hadn't yet begun her meal. With his mother and Harry, the three of them would just sit down and their food would be brought in for them to scoff as quickly as they could. There was nothing strict about mealtimes or the need to practice perfect manners, though their mother always insisted they use the napkins provided. And she did always insist they wash their hands before meals. But it was all fun. Even when William knew he was being cheeky or naughty, his mother would usually just roar with laughter and tell him to be a 'good boy', never giving him a piercing look or reprimanding him. William felt that he had to be on his best behaviour, even watching television at Balmoral or Sandringham sitting quietly and correctly on the sofa, not lying on the floor or on the sofa, with Harry by his side. And at home at Kensington Palace he could eat sweets or chocolate most of the time, though not before meals, but his mother would never let him eat too many at a time. And Diana never minded when they raced around the apartment chasing each other or playing games, often screaming and yelling in their enthusiasm. She would sometimes tell them to slow down or keep quiet or go to watch

Opposite page: Mischievous Prince William throwing stones in the river Dee at Balmoral, April 1987.

television, but always in a gentle, loving way and often with a smile or a laugh. Indeed, one of Diana's most endearing qualities was her inability to stop herself laughing and William and Harry would sometimes attack their mother, tickling her all over her body while she roared with laughter, unable to control herself as she tried to escape their prying little fingers. William loved those times with his mother and the times spent watching the Cartoon Network on the television, playing Sonic the Hedgehog, watching action videos with plenty of blazing guns, fast cars and tough heroes.

Above: Ludgrove Preparatory School.

Life with father was somewhat different. William felt in his younger days that his father was rather like a headmaster, telling him how to behave and what to do. His father didn't like him watching television, preferring that his sons read books for most of the time, although he approved of educational videos and some children's films. By the age of seven, William loved watching videos about dinosaurs, planets, space travel, wild animals and dangerous, poisonous bugs and insects. Wills would often go to his father for answers to all the hundreds of questions he had, whether it was about geography, wild animals, dinosaurs, other countries or how the stars stayed up in the sky. He also discovered his father was great company when they went outdoors together, particularly at Balmoral. He came to realise that his father was very knowledgeable about horses and hunting, shooting and fishing, stalking deer and understanding the countryside and each year he found himself becoming closer to Prince Charles, hoping that one day he would be as skilled in the knowledge and practices of the countryside. And he admired the way his father could make speeches

before hundreds of people without being shy or embarrassed and he wondered in his boyish insecurity whether, one day, he, too, would be able to deliver such speeches with the same confidence.

During the Easter holidays of 1993, however, a few months before William's eleventh birthday, a new person entered his life, someone of whom he took little notice at first but, within a matter of a few months, would become his best friend. Tiggy Legge-Bourke was a young woman whom Prince Charles wanted to help care for his sons when they were staying with him; someone who would become a friend to them, not an au pair exactly, but someone they could talk to without feeling embarrassed; someone who would almost become part of the family. Officially, Tiggy Legge-Bourke, who in 1993 was thirty years-old, was hired as an assistant to Charles's private secretary, Commander Richard Aylard. In reality, she hardly ever went near the office or was involved in any official work, but became a very modern nanny to Wills and Harry. She was paid £20,000 a year.

He found himself becoming closer to Prince Charles, hoping that one day he would be as skilled in the knowledge and practices of the countryside.

Within a few months, Tiggy had become a wonderful foil for the two boys and William became greatly attached to her, treating her as an older sister, someone he could tease, fight with and compete with, whether it was running, climbing trees or walking along logs. Tiggy, whose real name is Alexandra, was the quintessential upper-class girl, raised in the Welsh mountains on her parents' family estate, Glanusk Park, which occupies 6,000 acres around Crickhowell in Wales. She had first been educated at St David's Convent in Brecon, South Wales, an independent Roman Catholic school of 150 pupils run by the Ursuline order of nuns. She then moved to the Manor House in Durnford, an élite preparatory school for only fifty girls owned by Lady Tryon, the mother-in-law of Charles's old friend, Lady 'Kanga' Tryon. At the age of thirteen, Tiggy moved to Heathfield, Ascot in Berkshire, one of Britain's top girls' boarding schools, where she enjoyed herself immensely, excelling at netball and tennis. She was also extremely popular though not very academic, attaining only four 'O'-levels. It was ironic that Tiggy completed her education by attending the same exclusive Swiss finishing school as Princess Diana, the Chateau d'Oex, near Gstaad, the Institute Alpin Videmanette. Indeed, Tiggy would become a great companion for Wills and Harry, for she was not only extremely capable at tennis, lacrosse, netball and fencing but she was also an outdoor girl, enjoying swimming, riding, hunting, stalking, fishing and skiing.

Tiggy was also used to caring for young boys for, after attending a Montessori nursery-teaching course in London, she opened her own nursery in Battersea, South London, in 1985. It was named 'Mrs Tiggiwingle', the name she had chosen for herself simply because she loved the character of Beatrix Potter's famous hedgehog. Tiggy was a natural at caring for children, running a nursery, and her school for toddlers became very popular. Three years later, however, Tiggy's school got into financial difficulties and she was forced to close it. There was another good reason why Charles chose Tiggy as the companion for his sons – she was not exactly a fashion icon, as happy wearing jeans, Wellington boots and an old T-shirt and sweater all day as dressing up in an expensive outfit and high-heel shoes. Within weeks of taking the job, Tiggy earned the respect of William and Harry by teaching them how to shoot rabbits! They had no idea she was such a good shot.

William, Harry and Tiggy had great times together, and as William grew older he would try even harder to compete with Tiggy, challenging her at every opportunity. Indeed, when at Highgrove or Balmoral, William would plan their days together, giving himself the opportunity to test his developing skills at her expense. When they first met Tiggy in 1993, William was ten and Harry eight. Both boys loved having an older sister and they would often have mock fights together in their bedrooms or lounges when they would all scream with laughter and tussle with each other, William and Harry usually teaming up against poor Tiggy. But she was no shy violet and quite capable of looking after herself with two young lads. Within six months of her arrival, both William and Harry loved their time with her because they always had so much fun, whether it was kicking a football around, playing a little 'French' cricket, climbing trees or spending time trying to duck each other during friendly swimming pool fights. She also had a steadying influence on William who, at that time, had been dubbed 'the hooligan prince', as she channelled his enthusiasm and exuberant spirit towards a more outdoor, energetic life. Harry adored Tiggy, but the more time William spent with her, the more he would seek her advice, looking to her for explanations and sometimes confiding in her his concerns, such as the relationship between his mother and father.

Prince Charles was very happy that Tiggy had agreed to help out, for his sons and Tiggy always seemed to enjoy their time together, whether they were lying around on a sofa watching a video or, more than likely, enjoying some outside activity. But Tiggy didn't spoil the children, deciding what they were allowed to eat and not eat between mealtimes, so unlike their mother who loved to spoil them. 'I know I shouldn't spoil you boys,' Diana would tell Wills and Harry, 'but I can't help it; you're irresistible.' William enjoyed his time with Tiggy, especially the outdoor activities, but he became increasingly protective towards his mother. And yet William would, more often than not, seek Tiggy's advice, no matter what the problem, because he treated her as an older sister and, he believed, she understood his boyish problems more acutely than either his mother or father. As a result, William always sought her advice and, during the next five years, a remarkable relationship developed which would prove invaluable when the moment came when William really needed the comfort, support and love of a compassionate, strong, female figure.

'I know I shouldn't spoil you boys, but I can't help it; you're irresistible'.

When the boys weren't staying with their mother, they would nearly always be accompanied by Tiggy whether staying at Highgrove, Balmoral, Sandringham, at Klosters in Switzerland, sailing in the Mediterranean or, sometimes, at weekend house parties to which Charles had been invited. On those occasions, Tiggy would usually be provided with a bedroom next to Wills and Harry, and they would be her responsibility, giving Charles the opportunity to relax and enjoy the weekend with his friends. But Wills, Harry, Prince Charles and Tiggy would be at their happiest together at Balmoral where they would all go out together either shooting, fishing, riding or

*Above: William on one
of his first walkabouts at
Cardiff, March 1991.*

*Opposite page: William one
week after his seventh
birthday with Prince Harry.*

stalking. They would usually take a lunch with them and, come rain or shine, they would spend the entire day outdoors arriving back at the castle in time for a bath before dinner. William loved those days more and more, though he knew his mother disapproved of shooting and wasn't at all keen on riding, fishing or stalking. He grew to understand his mother's dislike of such country pursuits and would skate over the details of those activities whenever he phoned her from Balmoral for a chat. Once again, William felt he was only protecting his mother from facts she didn't really want to know and she was the last person in the world he wanted to hurt. William also came to realise that his father's relationship with Tiggy was far more peaceful than the weekends he recalled when his parents would stay together at Highgrove when tempers would flare and voices would be raised in anger. He had always sought to calm those situations, wanting his parents to enjoy being with one another. When staying at Highgrove for the weekend, Tiggy would have all her meals with Charles, Wills and Harry as if she was a member of the family; at dinner, she would usually share a bottle of wine with Charles and, as the boys grew older, Charles would allow them to enjoy the occasional glass. William liked the fact that the four of them would discuss so many different subjects during mealtimes and that there would be no arguments, no raised voices and no acrimony.

In Wills' mind, there was no one who could compare with his mother.

But William came to realise that his mother didn't seem to get on very well with Tiggy and he couldn't understand why. He noted that when he was relating some fun he had had with Tiggy, his mother didn't seemed to respond with her usual enthusiasm. Wills came to realise that his mother didn't want to hear of the great outdoor life he and Harry enjoyed with their soul-mate. When Tiggy began her job she would always pop into Kensington Palace for a chat with Diana but, after a few months, Wills noted that his mother had stopped inviting Tiggy into the apartment, preferring her to drop Wills and Harry at the door and not come in. The estrangement worried William because he had hoped that his mother and Tiggy would get on really well together, but it was not to be. He wondered why his mother seemed to be jealous of Tiggy, not realising that Diana felt that their nanny was stealing her sons' affection; that her boys were becoming more fond of Tiggy than they were of her. But in Wills' mind, there was no one who could compare with his mother, no one who could take her position in his life, no one who could take away the love he felt for her.

And, more than anything, William respected Diana. The more charity work she carried out, the more William admired her, almost idolising her as he watched people's reactions to his mother's kindnesses as she moved from one person to another, chatting, smiling to them. He would marvel at the affect his mother's presence had on patients in hospitals, old people's homes, orphanages, or those afflicted with ailments which kept them housebound. He would watch the people's eyes, see them light up at her approach and surely determined that, one day, when he became an adult, he might have the same effect on the less fortunate. But he never believed that he would be able to match his mother's touch of magic that seemed to transform people. He noted that his father didn't have the same effect on people and he wondered why. Whenever his mother gave William the opportunity to visit the sick or the disadvantaged, he would

Opposite page: With Princess Diana, St. David's Day, Cardiff 1991.

Princess Diana with William at Wimbledon, July 1991.

jump at the offer, because he simply loved to see his mother's reaction to people and the way those people reacted to her. Even when Diana took Wills and Harry to see teenagers and young people sleeping rough in London, begging for food or money, sleeping under cardboard in shop doorways or overcoming the effect of drugs, William would be amazed that however rude some of the young unfortunates were to his mother she would, for the most part, always win them over, so that after an awkward introduction and a few snide remarks, they would chat to her, talk of their problems, believing that Diana, Princess of Wales, was someone with the power to help them, who would indeed help them, even though she lived in a world far removed from them. And why? Because they trusted her. William hoped that when he came to undertake serious charity work, those sick, disabled and unfortunate people would also put their trust in him.

After Prince Charles 'retired' to Highgrove in the mid-1980s, William and Harry have looked to other men as father figures – not Diana's lovers, but a group of men happy to help out in the development of the young princes. Fortunately, there was no shortage of men willing to come forward and play the role of surrogate father, filling the emotional vacuum left by Charles when he moved his home and his office to Highgrove. Most of the time, William would only see these men for short periods, on occasional afternoons, perhaps, but, nevertheless, it meant that male role models were around during the prince's formative years. Jackie Stewart, the former world champion Grand Prix driver, was one such role model. He would take William and Harry to the British Grand Prix, escorting them around the track, introducing them to current top drivers, and answering their hundreds of questions about the cars, the drivers, the track and the art of driving at 200 mph. During one visit, William was allowed to sit in the seat of a Grand Prix car while Jackie Stewart explained everything to him. He loved that. King Constantine of Greece, a friend of the royals for many years, is one of William's godfathers and he takes a delight in caring for William, inviting him to his London home for occasional meals. Wills calls him 'Uncle Tino'.

He never believed he would be able to match his mother's touch of magic that seemed to transform people.

And there are two 'royals' to whom William has become very attached in the last few years – Viscount Linley, son of Princess Margaret and Lord Snowdon, and Peter Phillips, the son of Princess Anne and Captain Mark Phillips. David Linley, now 36, a trendy designer and cabinet maker, likes to ride around on sleek, powerful motorbikes and usually dresses in polo-neck sweaters, jeans, biker's boots and black leather jackets. William thinks his uncle David is ultra-cool and the two get on famously together. William has been to his uncle's workshop in Chelsea, ridden pillion on his bike and the two have enjoyed meals out together in the West End. In David, William had found a man young for his years with whom he could speak openly and honestly, who seemed to understand his problems. David's parents had also separated and divorced when he was a teenager. In 1991, David Linley accompanied Diana and the two young princes to Austria on one of their first skiing holidays, helping to introduce them to that difficult sport. One day, when William, then nine, broke down in tears, unable to keep up with young Harry, it was David Linley who cheered him up over lunch and persuaded him to have another go. Today, William is a very competent skier and each year loves to accompany to his father to Klosters in Switzerland, Charles's favourite resort. And then there is Peter Phillips, now twenty, whose parents finally divorced in 1992 after years of upset. Peter is very protective towards both William and Harry, with both boys regarding Peter Phillips as a sort of hero, someone to look up to and admire, who has played rugby for Scotland and lives an independent life. Peter volunteers to join William and Harry when they are holidaying at Balmoral. From his youth, Peter knows that life at Balmoral can be somewhat boring for young, adventurous, high-spirited boys, so he takes them off stalking, fishing and riding. They all get on really well together.

And then, of course, there is the man who is always close to William – his personal detective, the man responsible for his ultimate safety, who lives with him day and night, knows him better than his own parents. He almost never lets him out of his sights and is

He quickly earned the nickname 'Basher' because he was prone to punching his fellow school pals.

more often than not his closest friend, adviser, confidant and big brother, a man he can turn to whenever the going gets tough. William's first personal detective was Sergeant Ken Wharf, to whom William became so attached that Princess Diana asked that he should be moved to other duties. Since then, Sergeant Graham Cracker, now 44, a married man with two sons, has taken over and he now spends most of his life protecting William. Sergeant Cracker sleeps in an adjoining room to William at both Ludgrove and Eton, and tries to keep as a discreet a distance as possible from William when he is at Eton but, because the school is so open, Cracker must shadow him whenever he leaves the confines of the college. He will usually drive William, or, if there is a chauffeur, Cracker will sit in the front seat, ready for any eventuality. For most of the time, William gets on really well with the Sergeant but, on the odd occasion, his presence can sometimes upset the young heir to the throne. William was once chatting happily to an 18-year-old girl, but was convinced that Cracker could hear their conversation. So he went over to him and asked him to move twenty yards away. William was just thirteen.

But William has been no 'goody-two-shoes'. Indeed, quite the opposite. At Ludgrove, he quickly earned the nickname 'Basher' because he was prone to punching his fellow school pals whenever arguments broke out. Of course, teachers intervened as quickly as possible and the headmaster phoned Prince Charles asking whether he knew of any reason why William appeared to be so aggressive, far more so than any other pupil at the boarding school. Charles couldn't provide any explanation because William had never revealed such a trait at home. William also became very protective towards Harry when he joined him at Ludgrove and, if Harry found himself in trouble with any of his school friends, he would run to William for help. In an instant, William would respond, warning the other youngsters that he would become involved if they dared to tease or bully his younger brother. And because of the reputation Wills had built up at the school, his warnings were heeded. Such help and assistance forged a strong bond between Wills and Harry and, as a result, when Wills moved to Eton in 1995, Harry found life rather lonely without his big brother for company.

Just as William sought to protect his younger brother, so, from ten years of age, William wanted to protect his mother. One day he told Diana, 'When I grow up I'm going to be a policeman.' When she asked him why, Wills replied, 'So that I can look after you, of course.' Harry, however, promptly ruined Wills chivalrous ambition, remarking, 'You can't be a policeman. You've got be a king.'

William enjoyed his years at Ludgrove where he did well academically and felt proud when appointed a prefect in his final year. He only suffered one serious setback at the school and that was during the Easter term in 1993, when his school work deteriorated immediately following his parents' separation. But, with patience and perseverance,

Opposite page: William with the Beaufort Hunt, October 1994.

Left: At the British Grand Prix, July 1992.

Wills stuck to his guns and he passed his Common Entrance examination to Eton with flying colours. His Ludgrove teachers hoped that Wills would achieve a distinction, but he just missed out on that. At Ludgrove, he was kept behind a *cordon sanitaire*, a press and paparazzi-free zone. As a result, William, and later Harry, were able to lead remarkably ordinary lives, untroubled by the packs of photographers who would follow Diana whenever she set foot outside Kensington Palace. Such privacy permitted William to live a straightforward life at Ludgrove, enjoying a similar lifestyle as his friends without any royal favouritism. William showed himself to be intelligent, good-natured and popular with his peers. Despite his royal background, William showed no arrogance or precocious behaviour, and never pulled rank. To most of his peers, William was an average pupil, a fraction more popular than most other boys. The only

More than anything he wanted to prove himself and not be treated any differently

real problem he found at Ludgrove was that some of the teachers seemed to treat him as someone 'special' and he didn't like that because it made his friends jealous. More than anything, he wanted to prove himself and not to be treated any differently from any of the other boys. In his final year at Ludgrove, William was selected to read the lesson during the Christmas Carol service. Parents commented afterwards that William had shown 'considerable presence' with no hint of shyness. It was at Ludgrove that William learned how to play football, and he fell in love with the game. It was during football matches that Wills once again revealed his aggression, winning 50-50 balls, making hard tackles and was quite capable of looking after himself in any mêlée. During the holidays, he would persuade Tiggy to play football and Harry would tag along, too. In his final year at Ludgrove, William took great pride in representing the school at left full-back in matches against other schools.

At Ludgrove in particular, William fought to be treated like any other boy with no privileges. He didn't like the fact that his personal detectives had to keep watch over him day and night. Occasionally William would deliberately try to lose them. With the help of some friends, they would contrive to make Wills disappear, hiding him somewhere in the school or in the school grounds. That would cause immediate consternation, particularly amongst his bodyguards, but he didn't seem to care a damn. For a few minutes he was alone, able to do whatever he wanted without the close attention of one or more detectives. When William and his pals insisted on continuing their disappearing acts, the matter was referred to senior police chiefs who contacted Highgrove. Charles went to visit William and asked him to play the game, pointing out that the bodyguards had a job to do and it wasn't fair teasing them so much. Charles explained that if anything went wrong, the officers would be in the most serious trouble, and that wasn't fair to them. Reluctantly, Wills agreed, and his tricks stopped. But William came to detest the fact that he had to be chaperoned 24 hours a day. He was far happier at school when the detectives stayed in the background, out of sight, and a routine was worked out that made it possible for William to feel that he was on his own while, in fact, the detectives were able to keep an eye on their young charge. Wills resented the fact that, even on holidays overseas, he had to be chaperoned every waking moment, and at night he would often discover an armed detective asleep outside the door of his room! During one skiing holiday, he was sledging down a steep hill in the dark, along with other youngsters, and was seen to be careering towards a road at the bottom of the slope, where cars were driving slowly along. Seemingly from nowhere, one of the detectives looking after him suddenly appeared, threw himself on the speeding sledge and stopped it only yards before Wills and the sledge would have careered into the road. Wills and the detective ended up in a heap in the snow. William was livid. 'Why do I have to be surrounded by policeman all the time?' he shouted. 'I knew I was safe. Why won't you let me be a normal person?'

William enjoyed his carefree final year at Ludgrove. He was now a prefect, a member of the school soccer team and had gained a place in Ludgrove's cricket X1 during his last summer term. And he found himself rather enjoying his *exeat* weekends when he would spend two days and a night with either his father at Highgrove or with his mother at Kensington Palace. The weekends with his father would be quieter, more serious days, when they would often go for walks together and William would sometimes help his father in his prized walled garden. They would eat their meals together discussing everything under the sun and William would usually spend Saturday night watching a video. If Tiggy was at Highgrove, weekends were far more wild, action-packed occasions, when he would only see his father for meals while Wills and Tiggy spent their days outside riding, walking, shooting, playing football or tennis or going swimming. At Kensington Palace, life was far more relaxed for William, alone with his mother. Diana would try to arrange a visit to a museum, art gallery, cinema or amusement park, arrange for go-kart racing at which Wills excelled, showing great daring and skill. In the summer term, Diana and Wills might practice tennis at his mother's health club and William would often have some lessons with the club professional. Wills and his mother would sometimes go swimming together and he enjoyed fooling around with, ducking her, splashing her and trying to race her. Most of the time, however, Diana, who was a good swimmer, could easily out-swim her son but she would often let him win the races, to encourage his enthusiasm. If William wanted to eat out, Diana might take him to a McDonald's, but William would want to return home if any photographers showed up. But it was with his mother that Wills showed his teenage interests as he approached his thirteenth birthday. He liked action movies, science fiction and rock bands like Guns and Roses and Bon Jovi. He liked wearing black jeans, black T-shirts, bomber jackets and trainers, everything that he was not allowed to wear at Ludgrove or when appearing in public with his parents.

Why won't you let me be a normal person?

As William prepared to leave the protected life of boarding school at Ludgrove for the far more open, challenging society of Eton, however, he showed all the awareness of the the tough régime that lay ahead. As he had proved himself at Ludgrove, both on the sports field and academically, now he would need to show his true mettle, proving himself more capable and more competent than the boys he would compete against. He knew that Eton was an élitist establishment, the academic standards high. And yet the brief glimpses of William in those formative years revealed a young man capable of taking care of himself, with the manners of a young gentleman and the daring and courage of a boy who enjoyed pitting himself against his peers. He would need all those qualities to ensure he succeeded at Eton.

Chapter Three

'Youth's the season made for joys'

John Gay (1685-1732)

On June 21, 1995, Prince William became a teenager and, three months later, began life at Eton College, the famous public school on the River Thames at Windsor, founded in 1440 by King Henry VI. Before he arrived at the school in September, however, he had a good idea of what to expect because he had toured the college with his parents during the summer holidays, guided by the headmaster, New Zealander John Lewis; Dr Andrew Gailey, Master of Manor House; and the Matron of Manor House, Elizabeth Heathcote, who would become the most important woman in William's life for the duration of his years at Eton.

The 'Dame', as matrons are called at Eton, became William's surrogate mother, as she is to all the fifty boys in her care. She is responsible for dealing with all the emotional strains the boys may encounter, particularly the tougher, intensely competitive atmosphere of Eton which William discovered after only a couple of weeks at the illustrious college. Elizabeth Heathcote calls William by his first name, as do all the boys and teachers at Eton. All other boys are called by their surnames, but it was decided that William, should be called by his first name. He was welcomed by Dr Gailey, an Ulsterman in his late thirties, and his wife Shauna, as well as by Elizabeth Heathcote. He was shown to his room, a small study-cum-bedroom, which would be his 'quarters' for his five-year stay at Eton. His sole privilege is his own private bathroom, whereas all the other 49 boys in Manor House, a four-storey, ivy-clad building, have to share bathrooms. Dame Elizabeth, however, is the steady rock to whom all the boys turn for advice, sitting at lunch and dinner with the younger boys in the House while Dr Gailey sits with the older boys. Dame Elizabeth dishes out medicines and aspirins, signs 'chits' enabling the boys to buy on credit essential items like toothpaste, socks and stationery from local shops, billing parents at the end of each term. Above all, however, Dame Elizabeth would listen to any problems any of the boys might have; providing a shoulder to cry on, an adviser helping the younger boys to settle in to the unusual lifestyle at Eton. Dame Elizabeth, now 55, the daughter of an Old Etonian, has been at the school for nearly thirty years, is renowned for her kindness, warmth and sense of fun. Most weeks, Dame Elizabeth will invite a group of boys to her apartment to watch television, discuss some aspect of life at Eton and, most Saturdays, she holds coffee parties after lunch.

During that first term, Dr Gailey would sometimes knock on William's study door and drop in for a chat, checking how he was settling in, coping with everything, and how

*Opposite page:
A happy Prince
William with two of
his heroes, former
Formula 1 champions
Jackie Stewart and
Nigel Mansell,
British Grand Prix,
July 1992.*

Above: William at the wheel of a Formula 1 car, with tutor Jackie Stewart.

Opposite page: Getting in the mood, at Cardiff Arms Park, February 1992.

he was enjoying his new life. His wife would also invite some of the boys to her rooms for coffee or tea as they monitored the atmosphere in the House, encouraging the boys to enjoy living together in each other's pockets, eating their meals together, attending lessons together, and negotiating the mundane details of communal life. And, like every other boy, William had his own personal tutor, a Mr Stuart-Clarke, a young English teacher, who was charged with maintaining a continuous supervision over William's academic performance and intellectual development. For two hours each week, William would report to his tutor's rooms, chatting about his school work, his sporting interests and his relationships with other boys in the House. It was during these chats that William's 'order cards', report forms on which his teachers recorded his effort and attainment in class at three-weekly intervals, would be discussed. William was also invited to Mr Stuart-Clarke's home for informal evening meetings twice a week, sometimes with other boys, where they would all chat together over a mug of coffee or a soft drink.

Male role models were around during the prince's formative years. Jackie Stewart was one such role model.

Left: On the ski slopes
at Lech, Austria 1991.

Opposite page: William
the countryman, with
his young labrador
puppy.

Perhaps because of his successful years at Ludgrove, William did not find his early weeks at Eton as daunting or traumatic as many other boys in the House. He seems to have been well prepared for the rigours and idiosyncrasies of Eton life. But, like every other new boy, he was somewhat taken aback by some of the strange practices at Eton. Eton College is so very different from all other preparatory schools and, to a great extent, is quite different from most British public schools with all their traditions and protocol. Eton taught most subjects under the sun, including Latin, classical Greek, Arabic, Mandarin, Chinese and Japanese, as well as the modern European languages. But lessons are also provided in other subjects such as art, music, computer studies, cookery and car maintenance. William chose to play soccer and to row, but Etonians can also play rugby, cricket, tennis, fives and racquets, as well as the famous Eton Wall Game, a contest in which a wall is defended while the opposition attacks. There has been no score in this odd game for decades! The uniform at Eton is like no other in any British public school. The boys wear black tail-coats, a waistcoat, pinstriped trousers and a stiff white collar every day. When they walk into Windsor, however, they are allowed to wear ordinary, casual clothes. William is one among 1,260 boys (there are no girls at Eton) who live in twenty-four houses accommodating about fifty boys each. Fees cost £12,500 a year, but extras bring that total to around £15,000 a year! Eton used to be regarded as an élitist school, filled with plummy-voiced sons of the aristocrats, the upper classes, landowners, bankers and Tory grandees. To a great extent, all that has changed during the past twenty years and now Eton society is far more egalitarian. In the past decade, Eton has set its reputation on academia rather than snobbery. Until 1990, parents had to put down their son's name almost at birth to ensure entry, but this has since changed. Nowadays, places will only be promised when the child reaches eleven years of age and then only if they pass the entrance examination. Even William would, allegedly, have been turned down for Eton if he hadn't passed the exam, but fortunately he did very well.

One of the reasons why Eton was chosen by both Prince Charles and Princess Diana was because of the education system as well as the close camaraderie among the boys. Charles hated the years he spent at Gordonstoun, in Scotland, with a passion. There Charles felt bullied, estranged and isolated, and later referred to that period of his life as 'like a prison sentence'. Eton, on the other hand, is renowned for encouraging a friendly, family atmosphere as well as moulding the students' characters for life. There exists at Eton a unique pastoral care system, a complex network of people and informal relationships designed to ensure that no one slips through the net and no one's troubles go unnoticed. In Manor House, as in all Eton's houses, the housemaster always chats to boys around the house; his wife is always attentive to any of their problems; and, of course, there is Dame Elizabeth to administer to any immediate medical needs, which means that she is usually the first person to whom a boy is likely to pour out his heart. As a result, the great majority of boys find that the friendships they forge at Eton often last a lifetime. That is extremely important for William because it is unlikely that there will be other opportunities for him to establish strong friendships once he leaves Eton, for his life is likely to be ordered, if not pre-ordained, restricted by protocol and tradition. From his first weeks at Eton, William found a wonderfully ordered life, so very different from the existence he had been living, having to divide his time between spending time with his father and his mother, juggling the emotions of both parents, behaving differently in his two homes for life in both was so very different, which naturally placed a great deal of pressure on the young William's shoulders. At Kensington Palace, William dressed in a baseball cap, a shirt and jeans; at Highgrove he would dress more formally; and at Balmoral he would dress in a kilt!

From William's perspective, however, he discovered he wasn't the only privileged schoolboy at Eton. His grandmother might live in a palace; his father might be the heir to the throne; his mother might be considered the

William came to realise that, after Eton, he would never again enjoy such freedom of movement.

most glamourous woman of the age, but Eton also educates other boys whose parents live in palatial surroundings, own two or three homes in various parts of the world, fly around in their own planes and helicopters, and have their own servants and chauffeurs. A few boys even have their own bodyguards. And William also discovered over time that he wasn't the only boy at Eton who had had to live through the trauma of divorcing parents, although no other boys had to endure such a public marital split with graphic daily newspaper reports of the state of their marriage and the other parties involved. Prince Charles and Diana hoped that Eton would give William an unchallengeable air of self-assurance, something which both Charles and Diana singularly lacked at the completion of their education. William will also have a wonderful network of contacts and some close friends to whom he will be able to turn for advice, friendship and fun.

Of course, William had to be guarded by detectives at Eton because the entire college is easily accessible by public roads, creating major headaches for those involved in organising his security 24 hours a day. Fortress Ludgrove, as the school was known, set back from public thoroughfares, was virtually impenetrable without breaking trespass laws. As a result, William's and Harry's bodyguards at Ludgrove were able to give the royal children a great deal of space, and the detectives remained unobtrusive most of the time. Eton, however, is very different. Indeed, the senior Royal Protection Squad officers who surveyed the College declared the job to be 'a nightmare', for the entire school is so open and virtually impossible to police with just one or two armed men. Though William didn't like the prospect of being kept under constant surveillance at Eton, he understood that he could do nothing about it, and had to put up with it. And yet, when his father explained the necessity of security, William came to realise that, after Eton, he would never again enjoy such freedom of movement, the freedom to strike up friendships with whoever he wanted, and the freedom to come and go without hindrance. And yet whenever William left the confines of the school or Manor House to walk into Windsor for tea or to shop, usually accompanied by two or three school chums, two armed detectives would always follow. They would be dressed in smart suits, usually looking like businessmen, but in their shoulder holsters they were carrying Heckler & Kock machine pistols. The two bodyguards would always keep William in view, usually walking between twenty to fifty yards behind him. If the town was crowded with shoppers, or as often occurred during the summer months, with thousands of tourists, the detectives would cover William more closely, only permitting the heir to the throne to walk ten yards ahead. For his part, William would take no notice of the two men, but some of his friends found the experience somewhat eerie to start with. His good friends, however, soon grew to take as little notice of the armed escort as William.

For the most part, William retained his anonymity while walking around Windsor with his pals. Of course, he looked no different from any other young Eton scholar out for the afternoon, but as he grew older and his looks became more recognisable, more townspeople would have a second glance at the handsome, fair-haired, six-foot-tall young man with the ready smile, and realise that the young man was, indeed, William, the heir to the throne. Some townspeople would walk past and, say 'good luck' in a quiet voice so as not to attract attention. William would usually reply with a 'thank you' and keep on walking, for he had been advised by his bodyguards not to stop and talk to anyone on such occasions. Tourists, however, became far more adventurous as William's sixteenth birthday loomed and he became that much more recognisable. During his first summer at Eton in 1996, William was still very much a boy and, to strangers, no different from the hundreds of other young Etonians they saw out and about. Consequently, tourists from abroad and visitors to the town, who only had a sketchy idea of what young William looked like, barely had a clue as to William's identity. By the summer of 1998, however, photographs of William taken at his mother's funeral, during holidays and his visit to Canada, showed he had suddenly blossomed into a well-built, tall young man, so very like his mother, and he was far

Below: With his mother at the Wimbledon Women's final, July 1994.

Opposite page: Harry and Wills leave Chelsea Harbour gym after a game of tennis.

more easily identified by those who visited Windsor in the hope of seeing him. Those tourists who did recognise William during that summer term, however, only wanted to look at him rather than speak to him. Some would simply stare at him as he walked along the road, others would point to him, showing other people in their group who he was. But, for the greater part, they were reluctant to approach him and speak to him, seemingly fearful that they might be intruding on the young prince's privacy. In that way, they showed respect for William and the memory of his mother, for which William was very grateful.

William only reacted when people began taking photographs of him in the street as though they had a right to do so, simply because he was the heir to the throne or because he was Diana and Charles's son. Nothing enraged William more than people taking photographs of him. As if by instinct, William would react by ducking his head so that people couldn't see his face, or he would walk behind one of his friends using him as a shield. He didn't see what right they had to take photographs of him without permission, as though he was simply there for their benefit. His annoyance stems from the countless times he had seen his mother return to Kensington Palace, often upset and sometimes with tears in her eyes, simply because of the disgraceful antics of the scrum of paparazzi photographers who had chased and hounded her.

During his childhood, William didn't mind photo sessions, when a selected handful of photographers would be invited to take pictures of Charles, Diana and young William. On one occasion, when he could barely walk, William was quite taken with a television camera, examining it in some detail while the poor cameraman did all in his power to keep the young royal in focus. William came right up to the lens, looking at it from a few inches, causing much laughter and merriment from the royals and everyone else attending the photo session. During his early years he didn't seem to mind when cameramen and photographers took pictures of him and Diana walking along, attending polo matches at Windsor Great Park or at other functions. It was only when he realised the extent to which photographers hounded, frightened and upset his mother that William developed a deep distrust and loathing for cameramen which has so far lasted six or seven years. When William went skiing with Harry and his mother at Lech in 1995, he took on the role of protector, despite the fact that all three had armed bodyguards with them and their own detectives. But Wills noticed that, having agreed to take no more shots of his mother that day, a group of photographers had ignored the agreement and had begun to tail her down the slopes. William, a good skier for his age, immediately went over to the group and remonstrated with them, threatening to take away their cameras if they didn't leave his mother alone. The photographers were somewhat surprised at William's reaction and the situation was only resolved after William's personal detective skied over and reasoned with the young prince, after securing a promise from the photographers that they would go and away and leave the royal party in peace.

William has learned from a remarkably young age that there is no *quid pro quo* with the paparazzi or the tabloid press. He firmly believes, on a theory based on first-hand knowledge, that if an agreement is made to pose for a few pictures in return for being left alone for the rest of the day, the photographers will not abide by the agreement. He has found that, more often than not, they will still tail, shoot film, aggravate and invade the privacy of the royals if they think they can get away with it. It doesn't matter if such agreements are reached on holiday, on a ski slope, during a beach holiday or visiting a theme park, for William is convinced that the royal family can never trust the press. As a result, William refuses to play ball with photographers, deliberately making their job more difficult, if not impossible. As a result, William has for many years refused to keep to agreements made with the press, refusing, for example, to stand by Diana for a staged photo-opportunity because he just doesn't want to go along with anything that the press wants to organise. When photo calls are organised with the press, William will quite often refuse to take part, whether the photo-opportunities are during beach or ski holidays or even at Balmoral. And it was not only when Diana was around. During one famous photo call on the banks of the River Dee at Balmoral with his father and Harry, William made it very plain that he had no intention of posing for pictures. On that occasion, his father asked him to pose with him, giving him stern looks in an effort to persuade him to come and join the photo call, but William made it very obvious that he was not at all happy. When Prince Charles insisted that he

Nothing enraged William more than people taking photographs of him.

Opposite page: Watching the march past at VJ Day, August 1995.

Right: William, a keen sportsman, plays on, having injured his hand in a rugby match at Eton.

He had suddenly blossomed
into a well built, tall young man,
so very like his mother.

come and pose for the shoot, William obeyed, but most reluctantly, and, as a result, the photographs the pressmen sent back to their offices were of a poor quality. Superficially, the photocall on the banks of the Dee appeared to show William as a cheerful, gangly youth with a ready smile. The reality was that only a handful of frames from countless rolls of film shot by the assembled photographers showed what everyone wanted to see. The rest showed endless images of a gloomy William staring listlessly at his shoes; a sullen, unco-operative William wishing he was anywhere else; an unhappy William deliberately ignoring his father's coaxing to put on a happy face. Only the promise that he would be left alone in peace to enjoy the rest of his holiday at Balmoral finally persuaded him to co-operate. But his compliance was still grudging. Only twice did he briefly lift his head up to look directly at the cameras. It certainly didn't look as though William was enjoying his fishing holiday with his father, causing royal correspondents to write reams of copy about the 'unhappy' heir to the throne. William's behaviour on that occasion caused child psychologists to wonder why he had reacted so negatively. Most considered that the damage that Charles and Diana had inflicted on their elder son through their unhappy marriage was nothing short of catastrophic. They believed that Diana's *Panorama* confession and Charles' Jonathan Dimbleby interview were disastrous for William, revealing to the world that both his parents were untrustworthy and capable of making mistakes. Others believed that Diana's confession revealing details of her own sexuality and adultery, talking to the nation of such personal, intimate and delicate matters, caused the young, vulnerable, pubescent William shame and humiliation. As a result, William found every newspaper article about his mother or his father excruciatingly embarrassing

William is convinced that the Royal family can never trust the press.

In 1994, William was even reduced to tears when his father ordered him to pose for a group holiday photograph when enjoying a Mediterranean holiday on board the yacht *Alexander*, owned by the millionaire John Latsis, who has been a friend of the Royal family for decades. On that occasion, William slipped away as the group of holidaymakers took up their positions for the photo call but his presence was missed and Charles had to dragoon his son into returning. William was obviously deeply upset at having to obey that order and burst out crying. He could be seen desperately trying to brush away his tears as he finally obeyed his father and walked back to the group. But he was still determined never to pose again during that holiday, revealing the stubborn streak in his nature.

William's strong reaction to the paparazzi was not surprising. Not only had he witnessed the treatment meted out to his mother by photographers ever since he could remember, but he had also suffered at their hands. In the summer of 1996, Diana had booked a villa in the South of France where she intended to holiday with Wills and Harry and, of course, their accompanying private detectives. Unfortunately, the villa could be seen from woods about two hundred yards away, a public place where the family could be placed under constant surveillance by photographers. As a result, the holiday was ruined. The paparazzi discovered their hideaway villa and all but camped out in the wood. Night and day, relays of photographers from various photo agencies kept a vigil. Neither Diana, William nor Harry could venture out on to the terrace or to the swimming pool without the photographers snapping away with glee. Diana's detectives tried to persuade the photographers to leave the family alone, but they refused, saying they were only doing their jobs. In fact, there was nothing the detectives could do because the photographers were in a public place. William, however, became furious at the intrusion and could not understand why the photographers could not be sent packing. He appealed to his mother to do whatever was necessary to get rid of the photographers. But she knew from years of experience that nothing could be done to make them disperse, save for asking as politely as possible. And they refused. As a result, William stayed indoors during daylight hours, so determined had he become to thwart the paparazzi preying on the family. Harry didn't appear to mind the presence of the photographers and enjoyed his holiday, but he didn't like the fact that his older brother refused to leave the protection of the villa to play. As a result of William's anger and disillusionment, Diana thought it best to quit the villa early and return to London.

It was because of such awful experiences that William continued his private war against the press in general and photographers in particular. Of course, for much of the time after the troubles in his parents' marriage hit the headlines in 1990, newspapers were deliberately kept away from William to protect him. At Ludgrove, for example, when the boys would attend away football matches, the coach driver would take circuitous routes in a deliberate attempt to avoid newsagents who might have billboards outside their shops with headlines about the latest royal scandal. At Ludgrove, newspapers were heavily censored for the same reason and the tabloids banned. Indeed, at Kensington Palace, Highgrove and Balmoral, newspapers were kept in the background in an effort to protect Wills and Harry from the gory details of their parents' break-up.

During Wills' last summer holiday with his mother in July, 1997, at Castel Sainte Terese, Mohamed Al Fayed's villa in St Tropez in the South of France, the royal party were able to enjoy their two-week break without any interference from the paparazzi. No photographers were able to get near the Fayed villa. But when Diana, Wills and Harry ventured out to a beach or boarded Fayed's magnificent yacht, *Jonikal*, boatloads of reporters and photographers would close in on the royal party. Photographers armed with long-range lenses and reporters with high-powered binoculars caused distress, particularly to young William. He became angry and upset that the family could not enjoy a few hours by themselves without any press intrusion. That was the reason why Diana on one occasion took it upon herself to take a fast speed-boat to the reporters and photographers to plead with them to move away and leave the family in peace. They ignored the plea and, as a result, the family returned to the security of the villa. It was yet more confirmation in Williams mind of the need for a resistant to the pens and papparazzi.

He could be seen desperately trying to brush away his tears as he finally obeyed his father.

Only a few weeks later, William and Harry were with their father at Balmoral enjoying country pursuits. A photocall was arranged for the British press one August morning to picture Charles and his sons fishing on the River Dee. William, however, was not keen to take part, fed up with having to pose for press pictures when, only weeks before, the press had refused to co-operate during their St Tropez holiday. For more than an hour,

Above: Trying his luck at
Tetbury village fair, near
Highgrove, April 1995.

Opposite page: A pensive
William, at his grandmother's
ninety-seventh birthday,
Clarence House, London.

the photographers waited anxiously for William to agree to pose and, eventually, after pleas and explanations from his father, he agreed, but the photographs revealed William looking glum and depressed. He was fifteen and showing his true feelings, in the same way as his mother had done a hundred times when she had not wanted to pose for the inevitable massed ranks. On some occasions, however, William was prepared to pose happily for the necessary photograph. Such an occasion was his confirmation at Windsor Castle in March 1997 when, with Diana and Harry they sat smiling happily while selected photographers clicked away. But those occasions would be few and far between.

William enjoys the adulation, Canada 1998.

Even when he was much younger, William didn't appear to relish the idea of posing for pictures. During the Wales's official royal tour of Canada in October 1991, Prince William, then only nine years-old, didn't fancy posing for the official photo of the Royal Family with the crew of the Royal Yacht Britannia leaving for home. Instead of posing quietly, William decided to wave at the crowds on the quay below. His mother told him to keep still and stop waving, but Wills took not the slightest notice. So Diana slapped his arm quite hard, telling him, 'Do as you are told.' The naughty William, however, continued to wave earning himself another whack on the arm from Diana. He then went into a sulk. A few minutes later the Royal family should all have been together on the top deck waving goodbye to the crowds who had gathered. William, however, had disappeared. Charles disappeared from view, took hold of his son and told him to join the others immediately. A reluctant William walked sheepishly back to join the others, barely smiled and hardly managed a wave.

William, who is now adored wherever he goes, yearns to be anonymous.

Many psychologists believe that William has been scarred by the break-up of his parents' marriage and also by the public revelations of the intimate details of their respective lives. Some believe that before the death of Diana, William was showing signs of being profoundly affected by the persistent intrusion, walking around with his head bowed, hiding his face from cameras, giving the impression that he might actually fear the power of the camera lens. Some believe William is deeply suspicious of strangers, sometimes giving the impression of a hunted animal when he's not surrounded by friends or family. In July 1997, William was being driven by his father to watch a polo match at Windsor Great Park. As soon as William saw a group of cameramen, he immediately dived on the floor of the Aston-Martin, ensuring that they would not be able to capture a picture of him.

While many pre-possessing, handsome teenage boys rebel by trying to stand out from their peers, William, who is now adored wherever he goes, yearns to anonymous. That is the principal reason William is so happy at Eton. All the boys, including William, wear the same uniforms, attend the same classes, play the same games, and William is treated in exactly the same way as all the other teenage boys. Inside Eton, Wills feels protected, cut off from the outside world, shielded from the glare of publicity, and is provided with the stability he craves and the anonymity he loves.

Chapter Four

'The days of our youth are the days of our glory'

Lord Byron (1788-1824)

Throughout his teenage years, William was greatly influenced by his mother who was desperately keen for him and his younger brother, to grow up like normal, ordinary kids, experiencing as many facets of life as other teenagers. That was the reason Diana was seen dressing her boys in jeans, sneakers, T-shirts, bomber jackets and baseball caps; taking them to cinemas and go-karting; visiting burger bars; taking them on skiing and summer holidays. And that was the reason why Diana was happy for William to attend teenage dances, as well as taking them to visit the homeless and the disadvantaged. It showed the young Princes how fortunate they were to be living such a privileged life. Diana also hoped that they would follow in her footsteps, showing the same care and understanding to those less fortunate, with the same gentleness and empathy.

Princess Diana wanted to show her sons the other side of life; that it wasn't necessary to conform to protocol and tradition. She wanted them to be independent, to make their own decisions and not to be bound by the strictures of life within the Royal Family. Diana herself had always bucked the system, done her own thing, rebelled against protocol and tradition. From the first few months following her marriage in July 1981, Diana had shown a healthy dislike of the Royal way of doing things. She

Diana herself had always bucked the system, done her own thing, rebelled against protocol and tradition.

had fired many of Charles' staff; and demanded that she live the life she wanted without restrictions imposed by tradition. She had decided to have her firstborn delivered in a high-tech London hospital and not, as tradition dictated, in a room at Buckingham Palace. And from the first she made all the decisions, breast-feeding her own children, quite unlike royal tradition; insisting on naming her children herself rather than permitting the Royal Family to decide on the names. And she didn't simply let the nanny take over the care of Wills and Harry, insisting on doing many of the maternal jobs herself. Diana loved bathing and feeding Wills and Harry, cuddling and snuggling them in her bed in the morning; even changing nappies delighted her. Throughout their childhood, Diana was nearly always there for her boys, playing with them, feeding them, encouraging them, hugging and kissing them, so unlike the great majority of royal mothers. And from the moment of her separation in December 1992, Diana seemed more determined than ever to ensure that her boys grew up to understand and, if possible, experience the lifestyles of their contemporaries from as many different social backgrounds as possible.

Diana also introduced her close male friends to William and Harry. It seemed that she never tried to hide them away from her sons; in fact, rather the opposite, going out of her way to encourage contact with them, to involve her sons with the men she saw both during and after her marriage. James Hewitt, one of the great loves of her life, became a good friend to young William. Diana and Hewitt became friends in 1985, when William was just four years of age, and she and the handsome cavalry officer became lovers a year later. Hewitt began by giving Diana riding lessons in Windsor Great Park. Diana had lost her nerve as a ten-year-old when she was thrown from her pony, breaking her arm. Prince Charles and the Queen tried to encourage her to take up riding again, to instil the confidence she had known as a young girl when she excelled at the sport. But to no avail. The only person to instil the necessary confidence was James Hewitt. The young guards officer would give Diana riding lessons, take her out riding in Windsor Great Park and, slowly, Diana regained her confidence and her ability. As a result, Hewitt began to teach William, giving him greater confidence. Young Harry, on the other hand, needed no such help. A natural, courageous, even dare-devil horseman, Harry has a great natural ability. William and Harry would drive down to Windsor with their mother for lessons with Hewitt, while, unknown to the young boys, a strong physical attraction was developing between their mother and James Hewitt.

For the most part, William was totally unaware that his mother had become involved with other men.

Wills and Harry would also meet Hewitt when he called at Kensington Palace for a drink or a meal with Diana. Charles had moved down to Highgrove, removing all his clothes and his personal effects to his country estate. Sometimes, Hewitt would read the boys bedtime stories, play rough and tumble games with them in the drawing room at Kensington Palace and tuck them up in bed. At that time, of course, William had no idea that his mother was having an affair with Hewitt, whom the boys called by his first name. But as the months rolled into years, Hewitt became a constant and regular visitor at the palace and, on occasions, he would phone and chat to the boys asking how they were getting on at school and enjoying riding, swimming, tennis lessons and their latest favourite video. It was only later, when the press revealed that Diana and James Hewitt were lovers, that William began to realise that the kind, friendly, fun James had become a rival to him. William began to notice how much attention his mother paid to James whenever he visited their home; he noticed how long his mother spent on the phone to James rather than playing with him and Harry; and came to realise that his mother used to go away to spend weekends with him.

After James Hewitt there were others. For the most part, William was totally unaware that his mother had become involved with other men. He thought they were just good friends. William met the England rugby captain Will Carling and Oliver Hoare, an expert in Islamic art and antiques, who had been a friend of Prince Charles for many years. Though he was married to a lovely and beautiful wife, Diane, and with three children, Princess Diana fell completely and unashamedly head over heels for the handsome, sophisticated Hoare. He had tried to help patch up the royal marriage, but the more Diana saw of him, the more she became infatuated with him, until she found herself hopelessly in love. Oliver Hoare would visit Diana at Kensington Palace in the 1990s, and Wills and Harry didn't find that in the least strange because the Hoares had often been invited to Kensington Palace for lunch or dinner when Charles was also living there. As Diana's need for a shoulder to cry on became more desperate, the more Oliver Hoare would be invited to the palace to calm her and help her in her hour of need. Wills and Harry became quite used to seeing Oliver Hoare at their home. He would become another surrogate father to the two young princes. Diana's relationship with Will Carling, however, was a different matter, for not only was William very happy to see and chat to one of his heroes, he became somewhat star-struck at having such a celebrity as a regular visitor. William was in his element when Carling invited him to train one day with the entire England Rugby XV. William believed that his sporty mother and Carling were just good friends, little realising that they were enjoying a friendship of such intimacy..

No one can be sure how William reacted to the comings and goings of his mother's friends and confidants and, of course, for the most part, William was at boarding school, enabling his mother to enjoy her relationships in private without either of her sons realising exactly what the nature of them was. And yet William knew, perhaps instinctively, that whenever these callers were visiting, his mother would spend more time chatting to them than concentrating on him and his brother. The very fact of his parents break up, separation and divorce, caused William great heart ache and anxiety. It also put him through more emotional trauma than the average split because it was such a public affair, the entire nation being informed of every tiny incident on the front pages of the every newspaper. At school, he felt useless and redundant. William felt that he was forever in the middle of a tragic tug-of-love between his father and his mother. He reacted by trying to please both.

At first, William took it upon himself to provide the strength that he believed his mother lacked; always wanting to stay with her, protect her, care for her, so that she wouldn't feel so miserable. He would dress as his mother suggested, like all his pals at

William believed that his sporty mother and Carling were just good friends.

home on holiday, in jeans and sneakers and T-shirts and a baseball cap. He loved going with her and Harry to theme parks, to the cinema, to burger bars, to amusement parks, as well as to museums. But as he matured and became a teenager, William discovered that he rather enjoyed the company of his father and the country life pursuits around Sandringham and Balmoral where there were no cameras or journalists to ruin his day. There was nothing William enjoyed more than dressing in warm clothes, a Barbour and hiking boots and spending the day with Prince Charles stalking deer for hours on end, no matter how filthy the weather. In fact, the tougher the day out, the more William enjoyed himself, proving to his father that he was tough enough and strong

William with his father on the banks of the river Dee, Balmoral, August 1997.

enough to keep up with the rest of the party. And, furthermore, he began to prefer hunting, shooting, riding and fishing to the activities shared with his mother in London. And he didn't mind the fact that, with his father, he was expected to dress in a jacket, trousers and shoes, though he wasn't so keen on the strictures placed on him at mealtimes with his grandparents, having to arrive at exactly the correct time and behave with decorum and politeness, waiting to be spoken to. It was all so very different from the fun, informal and chaotic mealtimes at home with his mother and little brother.

And some time after his thirteenth birthday, in June, 1995, William discovered girls. As a young child he had always been somewhat precocious and, like many young boys, intrigued by girls of his own age. But from the start of his teenage years, William developed a far greater interest and fascination with the opposite sex. During beach holidays, he would often watch nubile young girls, far older than himself, darting in and out of the water, lying topless on beaches and by swimming pools. But at that stage he was just happy to look and see and ask questions. But in October 1995, he asked whether he could go to the 'Toff's Ball' at London's Hammersmith Palais, an annual event for teenagers of the rich and famous, attended by up to 1,000 youngsters. Such thrashes for public school boys and girls have been around since the 1960s. Alcohol, of course, is banned and there are adult chaperones who roam the dance floor checking on the behaviour of all the youngsters, many of whom take the opportunity to go wild. Many do, of course, consume alcohol, having either taken it from home, or buying it in supermarkets and off licences. They usually consume the drinks in groups on their way to the ball, throwing back neat vodka, the favourite, and chasing that with cans of beer. As a result, of course, many arrive at the ball a little worse for wear, if not actually drunk and disorderly. Many of the teenage girls also join in the drinking bouts. It is, of course, the recipe for a night of teenage mayhem when, often for the first time, girls and boys are thrown together without their parents being around. And they go wild. After similar events in the past, there have been photographs of near, naked teenagers, some having sex, and drunken, unconscious revellers. Prince Charles was against William attending the ball but, with the support of his mother, Wills persuaded his father to let him attend with a group of his pals from Eton. The result was a near disaster, though William apparently behaved with decorum , having been followed around the building for three hours by a conga-line of mini-skirted teenage girls. 'Give me a kiss', 'Let's dance' and 'Give me a snog' were but three of the requests repeated a hundred times to William that night. Some predatory Lolitas were even more aggressive, prepared to tussle with the four Eton pals who acted as bodyguards to William. Throughout, William smiled and tried to enjoy himself but it was all but impossible for him to relax. Wills did dance with a number of girls, those who were introduced to him by his Eton friends, but for the greater part, the dances were wild. No one witnessed the heir to the throne smooching or snogging. And he saw the dance through to the bitter end, leaving, with his pals at 2am. The ball was covered in all its horrific splendour in the tabloid press over the next few days and, as a result, William did not attend the annual ball again.

During beach holidays, he would often watch young girls, far older than himself, darting in and out of the water, lying topless on beaches and by swimming pools.

Above: Jet-skiing in St Tropez, July 1997. William's last holiday with his mother.

Opposite page: Photocall at Ballator, Scotland, August 1997.

Although not permitted to put up photographs of pin-ups, or anything else, on the walls of his 10-foot by 7-foot room at Eton, the boys are allowed to stick such pictures inside the door of their lockers. Inside William's locker are photos of *Baywatch's* babe Pamela Anderson and Cindy Crawford. Other stars to have graced his locker include Claudia Schiffer, and Emma 'Baby Spice' Bunting. From the age of thirteen he would always flick through his mother's magazines, which included both *Vogue* and *Cosmopolitan*. He was known to fancy the Playboy models, twins Shane and Sia Barbi, who are the living image of Barbie dolls. On one occasion, giggling and nudging a school pal, William summoned his bodyguard to survey a picture of a very sexy looking model. Diana sportingly tore the photo in half, handing William and his friend half each. Deadpan, William told her, 'It was only the top halves we wanted.'

But William was beginning to show a far greater interest in the opposite sex, wanting to chat to them rather than simply ogle magazine photographs. And, unlike many fifteen-year-old boys, he never seemed to be bashful in their presence. During winter skiing at Klosters in 1996, Wills began chatting to an attractive teenage girl while on the slopes and seemed smitten. For a while, they skied together and Wills suggested they return on the ski-lift for another down hill run. He invited her for a bite of lunch, too. But the girl was leaving the following day and they never saw each other again.

At the time, William was five years her junior! During the same ski trip, Wills was much taken with another teenager, the stunning 18-year-old Zoe Cody-Simpson, the daughter of an Army General. Zoe, who had more than a passing resemblance to Diana, was invited to join the royal skiing party and take lunch with them. For two days, Zoe and William skied together and both seemed to have great fun, William smiling and chatting as though to the manor born. During school holidays, William has increasingly been meeting his cousin Zara Phillips, Peter's sister, and Princess Michael of Kent's daughter, Lady Gabriella Windsor, both of whom are just one year older than William.

Polo at Windsor with Prince Charles, June 1997.

A few months later, in July 1996, Prince William, looking older than his fourteen years, made the front cover of *Time* magazine. 'Can this boy save the monarchy?' was the question posed by *Time*. The magazine wrote, 'If the Waleses have damaged the monarchy terribly, they may also have provided its salvation in William, the bright, likeable Prince, beginning to capture the public's imagination. As the divorce brings one act of the royal drama to an end, another one begins, with a fresh and appealing star.'

In November 1996, William was spending his half-term at Balmoral with his father when he shocked animal welfare supporters by shooting his first stag. Apparently, Wills was thrilled for he had brought down the stag with a single shot. And, when Wills, Charles and others members of the shooting party inspected the dead beast, Wills was 'blooded', smeared on the forehead with the blood of the dead animal, just as his father had been when he shot his first stag at Balmoral more than thirty years earlier. William, who has become a crack shot, felled the stag with a high-velocity hunting rifle from nearly 150 yards.

Throughout his young life, William has never been afraid to take the initiative, sometimes displaying a remarkable adult sensibility.

The death of the animal caused dismay among animal welfare groups, while hunters praised his sporting ability. Despite statements saying that William was only involved in a culling exercise, the animal welfare campaigners condemned the shoot outright and castigated Prince Charles for permitting his son to participate in the ritual of the killing. Despite the protests, however, the stag's head has now become a prized trophy, prominently displayed in one of the long rooms at Balmoral. As his prowess with the gun increased, William, often accompanied by Harry and Tiggy, went for long walks around Balmoral and Sandringham looking for rabbits to shoot. Usually accompanied by a qualified gamekeeper, the three will often return with ten or twelve rabbits in the bag.

Throughout his young life, William has never been afraid to take the initiative, sometimes displaying a remarkable adult sensibility – phoning San Lorenzo's restaurant at seven years of age to book a table for his mother and himself, to cheer her up; phoning cinemas to book seats at the age of ten; showing powers of leadership when playing football at Ludgrove; encouraging other players; or directing team members. It didn't, therefore, surprise his parents when, in 1997, William asked them not to attend the most important day in Eton's year – June 4 – Parents Day, because he felt the attendance of press and bodyguards might spoil the day for others. However, they were both taken aback when William, totally off his own bat, invited Tiggy to attend instead. Bemused, and not sure how to react, Tiggy phoned Prince Charles and asked what she should do. Charles told her to pack a picnic and some wine, and go. Tiggy took along one of William's great friends, William van Cutsem, 16, and together they sat on a plaid rug on Agar's Plough, one of the Eton playing fields. They ate pâté, sandwiches, crisps and fruit and drank wine. They were also joined by three mini-skirted teenage girls who stayed to chat for fifteen minutes. After lunch, Wills and his friend went walkabout, moving from party to party, chatting to Eton pals and their parents and were introduced to scores of pretty girls, sisters and friends of friends. Dressed in his Eton uniform coat and tails, William was in great form, smiling, shaking hands and chatting to the girls he met. The teenage boy was rapidly becoming a young man.

Chapter Five

'The measure of our torment is the measure of our youth. God help us, for we knew the worst too young'

Rudyard Kipling (1865-1936)

Prince William was holidaying at Balmoral in Scotland with Harry, Prince Charles, the Queen and Prince Philip, when the tragic death of his mother occurred. The appaling crash in the tunnel beneath the Pont de l'Alma beside the River Seine in Paris happened at11.30 pm British summer time on Sunday, August 31, 1997. William and Harry were sleeping peacefully, having gone to bed before 10 pm that night, when the initial details of the crash were first telephoned to Balmoral. The devastating news that Diana, Princess of Wales, had been involved in a car accident was passed through the usual government channels, according to protocol. The duty officer of the French Interior Ministry telephoned his counterpart at the British Embassy in Paris some-time after 1 am French time. In turn, he immediately called the duty officer at the British Ambassador's residence in Paris who woke the ambassador, Sir Michael Jay, informing him of the accident.

At that stage, it was understood that Diana had only been injured and that none of her injuries were life-threatening, but French police had confirmed the deaths of both her travelling companion, Dodi Fayed, and the driver of the Mercedes, Henri Paul. The news of the accident was flashed from the British Embassy in Paris to the Foreign Office duty officer in London, who, in turn, called Buckingham Palace, giving the few details then known of the accident. However, as French doctors reported their serious worries about the extent of Diana's injuries, the decision was taken to telephone Balmoral and suggest that Prince Charles should be woken and informed of what had occurred. The duty police officer at Balmoral, who also doubled as duty night telephonist, took the call and phoned Charles' valet.

Shortly after 2.00 am, the duty valet knocked on Charles' bedroom door and told him what had happened. Charles immediately phoned Buckingham Palace and asked to be kept informed, directly, of any developments. He spoke to Sir Robert Fellowes, the Queen's Principal Private Secretary, Diana's brother-in-law, who was staying at Balmoral that weekend and, together, they came to the decision only to wake and inform the Queen if Diana's condition deteriorated further. One hour later, the news came through that Diana had died. It was 3 am. Charles was wide awake, sitting by the phone, for he had feared that further bad news might come through that night. But even he was not prepared for the news of her death. He was shocked, stunned that something like that could have occurred to Diana who was always so careful when driving, always wearing a seat belt, never taking risks on the road and never driving too

William on the Royal Tour of Canada with his father, skiing in Whistler, March 1998.

fast. He immediately phoned his mother, telling her of the appalling tragedy. He dressed quickly and went to the Queen's bedroom, telling her the scant details. After Charles had told his mother everything, the Queen phoned Prince Philip, telling him of the tragedy and inviting him to come and hear what Charles had to say.

What concerned all three was how and when the news should be broken to Wills and Harry. There was grave concern as to how Harry, only twelve, would cope with the terrible tragedy, and so it was decided that the boys, who slept in adjoining bedrooms, should not be given the devastating news of their mother's death until they had woken as usual at around 7.30 am. Charles shaved, showered and dressed before 7 am so he would be prepared and ready for the ordeal of telling his sons what had happened to their mother. After the two young princes had been awake for fifteen minutes or so, Charles went to see them in their rooms. He told them all he knew of the accident, he told them directly that Diana had died, along with her friend Dodi Fayed. No further details of that chat are known but, immediately afterwards, Charles took the boys to see the Queen and Philip who were also dressed for the day. For twenty minutes, William and Harry, with Charles, the Queen and Philip, discussed the matter and comforted the boys.

Charles telephoned Tiggy Legge-Bourke, the young woman who had won the affection of the two boys since having been appointed their unofficial Girl Friday in 1992. When Charles phoned Tiggy, shortly after breakfast on that fateful Sunday, and told her of the dreadful news, she immediately offered to fly to Scotland to offer whatever help and comfort she could to Wills and Harry. Charles was greatly relieved because he knew that of all the people the boys knew well, Tiggy was closest of all, closer than any aunts or any other members of the Royal Family. Charles also realised that, with Tiggy, the boys would be totally natural, and would not have to act courageously, bottling up their feelings. She would be able to talk to them, encourage them to release all their emotions, because they knew, and had known for some years, that Tiggy cared for them.

Charles encouraged William and Harry to accompany him to breakfast, the one informal meal of the day at Balmoral when the Queen permits the family to arrive in the dining room at whatever time they wish, helping themselves to whatever they want from a table at the side of the room. Footmen serve tea or coffee and will take any particular order, like bacon, eggs and mushrooms but, in the main, everyone grabs whatever they want and returns to their seats around the table. On that fateful Sunday the Queen and Philip also made the effort to come down for breakfast, joining William and Harry so they would feel they were in the bosom of their family. After breakfast, Charles asked his sons whether they wanted to go church that Sunday morning and stressed that if they didn't want to attend, if they didn't feel strong enough, then everyone would

Charles went to see them in their rooms. He told them all he knew of the accident, he told them directly that Diana had died.

understand. Harry looked at William who looked at his father and asked if he was planning on attending the morning service. It was, of course, a tradition of the Royal Family that whenever they stay at Balmoral the entire family attends Crathie Church, the small, local church near Balmoral every Sunday. Charles said that he intended to

accompany the Queen and Prince Philip and William said he, too, would like to go. Harry promptly said that he, too, wanted to go with his father and his brother. Dressed in grey suits and black ties, William and Harry sat either side of their father for the short car drive to and from the church. Their faces were almost expressionless and the parishioners, television cameramen, photographers and journalists who gathered to see the family were amazed to see neither William nor young Harry shed a tear. The composure of both boys was remarkable, revealing how, in a matter of just three hours, they had managed to shed their tears and then, somehow, cope with the pressure of appearing in public without breaking down.

But throughout that awful Sunday and the days that followed, both William and Harry would break down in tears from time to time. During that first week, William and, more frequently, Harry, would sometimes burst into tears as the awful truth of the tragedy washed over them. On those occasions, both Charles and Tiggy would comfort them, sometimes just putting an arm around them as they walked in the grounds of Balmoral, not needing to say a word, but just handing them a handkerchief to wipe their eyes, giving them time to gather themselves once more.

Above: On holiday in Canada with Prince Charles and Harry, March 1998

Opposite page: Attending the premie of Spiceworld in London, December 1997.

The scenes at Balmoral during the days following Diana's death were, understandably, traumatic for everyone, but particularly for William and Harry. The Queen and Prince Philip tried, in their own ways to comfort the boys, but there had never been a close, nurturing relationship between the boys and their paternal grandparents. The Queen's strong, reserved character had been forged in an earlier generation and even her own children would confess in their maturity that their mother had never been a maternal, warm-hearted person to whom they could turn for tenderness, though they all respected her for the work and the commitment she showed to the monarchy. Philip had been even more distant, for the most part treating his three sons as junior midshipmen rather than young boys needing help, advice and support. Charles understood this only too well – he didn't want to leave his sons alone at this distressing time, and yet he knew it was his duty to fly to France to recover Diana's body, though it meant leaving William and Harry at Balmoral. Before flying out, he discussed the matter with his sons, explaining why he had to go and they understood. Before he left, however, he promised to return to Balmoral to be with them that same night. William told his father that he understood, that he thought it right and proper that Charles should go to Paris. Indeed, William volunteered to accompany his father to France and return with his mother's body but Charles asked him instead to stay behind to care for Harry until Tiggy arrived. William agreed.

'Overnight, William became a young man. He even seemed to grow in stature ...'

Charles told his sons that if Diana's brother Charles Spencer had been living in England, then it would have been quite in order for him to fly to Paris and accompany the body back home, along with Diana's sisters. But as he was then living in South Africa there was no way he could make Paris in so short a time. Both William and Harry understood the predicament and they both told their father they were happy that he wanted to carry out the task. Both lads felt that their father had jumped at the opportunity to be close to their mother, the woman he had divorced. Now, it seemed to William, that in death his parents were to be far closer than during their life and that one, single, deliberate act brought William closer to his father. Charles's decision to take charge of everything, to care for Diana in her death, had a remarkable impact on William's relationship with his father. From that decision grew a bond between Charles and William which has become stronger than anything between them during the years that Diana was alive. In those days leading up to Diana's funeral and beyond, young William's relationship with his father changed dramatically and he felt closer to his father, more respectful and he felt acutely the love his father had for him.

During that first day at Balmoral, especially when Charles had to leave for Paris, young Harry became emotionally distraught and, before Tiggy arrived to comfort and look after him, William took on the responsibility of the big brother role. During that Sunday, Harry was inseperable from his brother and William seemed to mature almost overnight. William decided everything that day, taking all the decisions which Harry was happy to follow. And that was a dramatic change of character for Harry who is known as a most independent young boy, usually far more independent of spirit than William. Diana used to say that, before reaching a decision, she could always discuss matters with William, but Harry preferred to take instant decisions without consultation, wanting to do whatever he pleased, rather than discussing what everyone wanted to do.

William decided that they should play games inside, go for walks together in the autumn sun and kick a football around. William realised that he had to keep Harry's mind occupied, to stop him thinking of their mother and of her appaling death. As one stalwart of the Royal Family who has worked for them for thirty years commented, 'Overnight, William became a young man. He even seemed to grow in stature, taking command of Harry in a remarkably warm fashion, walking around the estate with his arm around his shoulders, talking to him whenever the tears flowed, comforting him, urging him to think only of the wonderful times they had together with their mother.' But Harry could not be comforted and throughout the first couple of days, he would simply ask, over and over again, 'Why? Why? Why did she die?'

At night, William would ensure that Harry was asleep before he went to bed, even though both his father and Tiggy were at Balmoral to care for Harry. But after the arrival of Tiggy, William became more introvert, despite the strong relationship he had always enjoyed with Tiggy, whom he had always treated as an older sister. Harry needed Tiggy's warmth, her open arms, her gentleness and her understanding. For much of that first week Harry spent the days walking around Balmoral with Tiggy and in the evening he would sit with her, cuddling up to her, needing her emotional stability and quiet strength. And William spent those days close to his father; chatting together as they had hardly done before, going for long walks around Balmoral, simply spending time together. And William gained emotional strength from his father, enabling him to come to terms with the death of his beloved mother. Charles would just let William chat away about anything, letting all his emotions run their natural course. Twice they went fishing together, fly-fishing, a sport William enjoys for the same reasons as Charles – it involves days alone by a fast-flowing river, away from the cares of the world, alone with one's thoughts.

Prince Charles wanted to involve both William and Harry in drawing up the details of their mother's funeral. Their uncle, Charles Spencer, along with their aunts, Jane Fellowes and Sarah McCorquodale, had said they also wanted to be involved in planning their sister's funeral because they felt Diana would not have wanted a staid, royal funeral full of protocol and historic precedence. Prince Charles discussed this with William and Harry and they both agreed that, if possible, their mother's funeral should reflect her life, the people she respected, the charities she helped rather than a church full of dignitaries, titled families, ambassadors and politicians whom she hardly ever met and, in her lifetime, didn't have much time for. And Charles Spencer, Jane and Sarah also wanted a special, extraordinary funeral service for Diana and they wanted to talk through all the plans with Wills and Harry.

William quickly became convinced that it was the paparazzi who were responsible for the accident and, therefore, her death.

Throughout that first week, both William and Harry seemed riveted to the television screen, wanting to learn all they could of the death of their mother. Together, they would watch as many news items as they could, hoping to learn something new, something that might throw light on how and why their mother had died. William quickly became convinced that it was the paparazzi who were responsible for the

*Opposite page:
Vancouver, Canada,
March 1998.

Below: William on the
Thames, May 1996.*

accident and, therefore, her death. Over the years, William had developed a loathing for the paparazzi, indeed, any photographers, who dogged Diana every time she ventured out of Kensington Palace. William had seen his mother break down in tears when chased by the photographers; he had seen the effect chasing cameramen had on his mother when she would arrive home, her make-up smudged, the tears drying on her cheeks, her emotions almost at breaking point. Since the age of twelve, William had come to hate the paparazzi with a vengeance and both Charles and Diana needed, from time to time, to tell him that the press, the newspapers, the television stations and the paparazzi were the link between the monarchy and the people, the messengers whose job it was to inform the nation of royal matters. For the most part, William understood this but he could never forget and would never forgive the behaviour of the rat pack that chased, dogged and humiliated his mother at every conceivable opportunity.

William convinced himself that the paparazzi were totally and completely responsible for his mother's death. He believed that if the photographers had not been chasing his mother that night there would have been no need for the chauffeur, Henri Paul, to race at speeds in excess of 100 mph through the streets of Paris and, therefore, there would have been no accident, no crash. And his mother would still be alive. Ever since the accident, no one has been able to persuade William otherwise. There is in William the

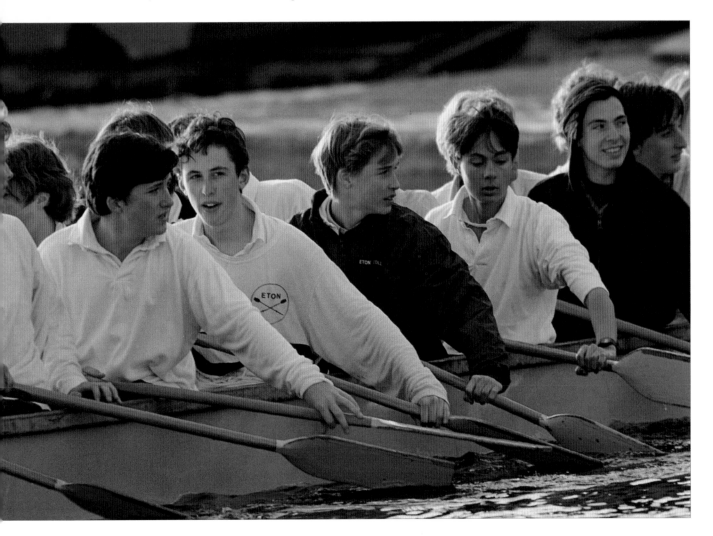

same stubborn streak that was part of Diana's character and, no matter what people might persuade him to say or do or accept, young William will come to his own conclusions and stick to them. Throughout her life, Diana showed she could be wonderfully stubborn, especially when senior Buckingham Palace courtiers would try to advise her, telling her how to behave or what to do. Diana would listen to what they had to say, often nodding in agreement – and then she would go and do exactly what she wanted, taking no notice whatsoever of the advice the courtiers had given her. Indeed, Diana would sometimes behave in exactly the same way with Charles, especially when their marriage was falling apart in the 1980s. Diana would come to an arrangement, or an agreement, with Charles and then happily go and do whatever she wished without even informing Charles that she had no intention of carrying out the agreement they had reached. And that, Diana knew, infuriated him.

Also during that week, William watched the television news bulletins and special programmes with amazement as the nation poured out its heart for his mother. William had some idea that his mother was the star of the royal family; he knew that whenever she appeared in public, women, in particular, would turn out to cheer her, even in the pouring rain. William knew that his mother had built up a special relationship with the British people and, on the few occasions he had accompanied his mother on official or unofficial engagements, he would see for himself the reaction of the people to his mother's presence. To William, there seemed a magic affinity which he could not quite understand. He had seen the general public react to his father but there had never been such a spontaneous outpouring of emotion, almost of love and affection, as the public showed towards his mother. Now, as he sat in front of the television at Balmoral, William realised just how close his mother had come to the British people, revealing an extraordinarily, deep relationship. It did not seem to matter that the hundreds of thousands to flocked to London to pay their respects to his mother had never met her, and most had never even seen her in the flesh. But, his mother had overcome that hurdle. As the television showed footage of her life, William came to understand, for the first time the relationship that had developed between his mother and the British people.

The same people who now flooded into London with their bunches of flowers, their messages of grief and their tears were the same people who had also wept tears at his mother's magnificent wedding in 1981; the same people had watched his mother's progress, enraptured by her smile and her kind, caring nature. They had felt happy for her when she gave birth to William and then, two years later, to Harry. They had watched the sparkle go out of Diana's eyes, watched her grow thin, painfully thin, and they understood that something was not right in her marriage. They saw the signs and they worried for her as if she was one of their daughters or a close friend. There was nothing they could do but show their support for her whenever she appeared in public. But when news leaked out that Charles had been seeing, Camilla Parker Bowles, the sympathy for his mother turned to anger for many of those cheering, sympathetic women had also suffered similarly miserable marriages and they understood the hell that Diana was going through.

During the week following his mother's death, when William seemed almost glued to the television screen, he learned more than he had learned throughout his life of the extraordinary relationship between his mother and the British people. He watched the television footage of his mother's remarkable progress from being simply the young mother to the heirs to the throne and wife of Prince Charles to a quite outstanding, international icon of the late twentieth century, a woman who had been left by the man she loved, who had suffered the agonies of anorexia and loneliness but who had shown extraordinary strength of character to give her life to others less privileged. It was during this harrowing week that William learned for the first time the extent to which his mother had been loved by the entire nation. He came to understand how his mother had won over the great mass of the British people, and many others worldwide, because of her tireless charity work, her dedication to the disadvantaged, the homeless and the underprivileged, to lepers and orphans, to cancer patients, AIDS victims and those maimed by landmines. And she had achieved this by the manner of her charity work, giving of herself to those she came to visit, loving them, holding and touching them, talking to them, showing her warmth and her concern. She had touched a chord in the nation and had won not only their respect but also their admiration and, more importantly, their love.

And William was also moved by the thousands of children who came with their parents to lay flowers, leave cards and, sometimes, their favourite teddy bears and dolls for his mother, wanting to give something of themselves. William was affected by the thousands of people who happily waited for hours simply to sign a book of condolence for his mother; who brought armfuls of flowers, and sometimes just a single flower, to show their love and reveal their grief, a river of people standing in stunned silence with but one simple mission, to show their love. Almost spellbound, William could not leave the television screen, taken aback by the overwhelming scenes he was witnessing. He was amazed at the open displays of grief, the quiet sobbing of so many people, who happily revealed their suffering and their sorrow in scenes which London had never before witnessed. The stiff upper lip which he knew his father and grandfather, as well as his friends at Eton, still believed in, and which William understood to be a part of the British character, had gone, to be replaced by open displays of grief.

William learned for the first time the extent to which his mother had been loved by the entire nation.

Most of the time William sat alone in front of the television that week, taking in everything the news bulletins covered in the greatest detail. From time to time, Tiggy and sometimes Harry would join him, but they were not so keenly interested in dissecting each and every piece of evidence that was examined by the journalists and experts. William could not be dissuaded from his firm belief that the principal reason for the crash was the chasing pack of photographers. He understood that the chauffeur should not have been driving while under the influence of drink; he understood that Henri Paul should not have driven at such excessive speeds; and he understood that his beloved mother should have been wearing her seat belt. William found it unbelievable that his mother wasn't wearing a seat belt that night, for she had always been strict about wearing a belt when she was driving and would never even permit a car to move away unless she had checked that her sons were correctly belted in their seats. Always, always, Diana herself would check their belts or she would ask the police officer travelling with them to check them. William found it difficult to believe that his mother would set off without her seat belt fastened or, even more extraordinarily, not secure the belt when she felt the excessive speeds at which they were travelling that night. William would talk to Tiggy about all these matters which were not debated to any great degree on the television, simply because he knew his mother so well; he knew how thorough she had always been.

William would stay up late during that first week, wanting to savour every moment of television coverage as the mood of the nation was captured. He wanted to go to London to mingle with the people who had showed so much love for his mother. On her behalf, William wanted to thank them personally, each and every one of them who had made the journey to London with their flowers, their cards, their messages and their gifts for his mother. William knew that his mother would have been amazed at the outpouring of tears and affection for her at the time of her death and he wanted to be a part of it. He wanted to join the all-night vigils in the royal parks; he wanted to queue with the ordinary people who sometimes waited for eight hours or more simply to write a few words in one of the thirty books of condolence that were required to cope with the demand. William wanted to be a part of the people's grief, sharing at first hand their sorrow and their torment. He understood that, like him, many who came to London were suffering from the sort of intense, personal grief that people usually experienced only after the sudden and unexpected loss of somebody close. Many of those who felt compelled to flock to London to show their love knew so much about Diana, by reading of her life, her problems, her sadness and her loneliness, that many had come to believe that they knew her extremely well. The fact that Diana was so young, so beautiful, so vulnerable and a mother, heightened the grief.

William wanted to go to London to thank everyone for the gifts of flowers they had brought, but the decision was taken by the Queen that this would not be appropriate for a young prince, barely fifteen years old, to lead the rest of the royal family in such a show of private grief in such a public manner. By the middle of the week, however, there were growing rumbles of discontent among the mourners and it was trumpeted by the tabloid press that the Royal Family had not shown sufficient public grief over Diana's death. The public would not be placated by statements from Buckingham Palace and Downing Street that the Royal Family were mourning in private, supporting William and Harry in their hour of need. William continued to press his father to be permitted to meet the mourners in London, to shake their hands, thank them personally and share their grief for his mother.

'It would appear that every proprietor and editor of every publication that has paid for intrusive, exploitative photographs ... has blood on their hands today.'

William actually cheered his uncle, Earl Charles Spencer, when he heard the statement he read out to the world before flying to London from his home in South Africa. 'All those who have come into contact with Diana,' Earl Spencer said, 'particularly over the last seventeen years, will share my family's grief. She was unique. She understood the most precious needs of human beings, particularly those who suffered. Her vibrancy, combined with a very real sense of duty, has now gone forever. It is heartbreaking to

lose such a human being, especially as she was only thirty-six. This is not a time for recriminations, but for sadness. However, I would say that I always believed the Press would kill her in the end. But not even I could imagine that they would take such a direct hand in her death, as seems to be the case. It would appear that every proprietor and editor of every publication that has paid for intrusive, exploitative photographs of her, encouraging greedy and ruthless individuals to risk everything in pursuit of Diana's image, has blood on their hands today.'

Both William and Harry waited at Balmoral for their father to return that night. They had watched live television pictures of the Queen's Flight landing at RAF Northolt in West London, bringing the body of their mother back home. They watched almost spellbound as their mother's body was taken from the aircraft, the coffin draped in a Royal Standard, and a ten-man bearer party from the Queen's Colour Squadron of the RAF Regiment escorted the coffin from the aircraft to the waiting hearse. No one can know what thoughts passed through their minds at that moment, for this was the first time that they had seen real evidence that their mother had indeed died. Tiggy sat with them, replying to Harry's questions which, for the most part, she was was able to answer, though she was no expert on protocol and procedure. After the hearse had driven away under police escort, the boys saw their father climb aboard the aircraft for his return flight to Scotland. Three hours later, he arrived back at Balmoral, and William and Harry greeted him as though they had not seen him for weeks. That night, more than any other night, William and Harry needed their father to be close to them. Shortly after 10 pm, Wills and Harry went to bed; it had been, by far, the longest day in their young lives.

When Earl Spencer arrived at Balmoral two days later, on Tuesday, September 2, along with aunts Lady Jane Fellowes and Sarah McCorquodale, the Queen had already decided that she would like the Spencer family to be intimately involved in planning Diana's funeral. It is customary in royal circles that funerals of members of the Royal family are enshrined in strict protocol, something which Diana fought against all her life. So the Queen suggested that Prince Charles and Earl Spencer, together with Diana's sisters, Jane and Sarah, as well as both William and Harry, should form a committee to plan and oversee the funeral details, as well as the church service. Sir Robert Fellowes, the Queen's Principal Private Secretary – William and Harry's uncle by marriage – would also sit on the committee to offer advice and represent the Queen's views.

William was particularly happy when he heard that Elton John had agreed to sing a new version of 'Candle in the Wind.'

The committee, with William and Harry in attendance, met on the Tuesday and Wednesday of that week. Sometimes, they asked advice from other people, and Sir Robert Fellowes was in constant contact with Prime Minister Tony Blair's senior officials at Downing Street. Tony Blair offered to help in any way he could and asked to be kept informed of the plans for the funeral service. Police chiefs in London were also involved and were asked for their advice on the route the funeral cortège should take and the necessary safety measures that should be implemented to take care of the million or more people expected to flock to London to show their last respects to the princess they adored. William and Harry were both invited to participate in the planning and, before any decision was taken, William, in particular, was asked for his views, and was asked whether his mother would have approved of the proposed plans. And all these questions were asked of William before any final decision was taken. For the most part, Harry would look for guidance from both William and his father, but William became increasingly involved in the planning, putting forward ideas and commenting enthusiastically whenever it was suggested that protocol would not be observed.

William was especially happy when the suggestion was made that representatives from Diana's favourite charities should be invited to attend the funeral service in Westminster Abbey rather than statesmen, politicians, ambassadors and representatives from other countries. And he liked the fact that friends, personal and close friends, of his mother's should be personally invited and given pride of place in the Abbey for he, perhaps more than anyone, realised that Diana had always put great store by ensuring she kept up her relationships with non-royal friends. William was also particularly happy when he heard that Elton John had agreed to sing a new version of 'Candle In The Wind', because he knew his mother loved that simple, moving song.

William was relieved when, five days after Diana's death, the Queen finally decided that the Royal Family should make a public appearance, but not in London. On Thursday, September 4, the Queen and Prince Philip drove to the gates of Balmoral Castle and inspected the flowers placed there by people from nearby villages. The Queen agreed to Prince Andrew and Prince Edward making an impromptu walkabout along the Mall in London and signing the book of condolences. They were the first members of the Royal Family to appear in London before the grieving nation. The Queen also agreed to make an unprecedented television address to the nation and

In young William's heart beat the same disdain for empty pomp and ceremony as that which drove his mother for so many years.

announced that Diana's funeral service would be a 'unique funeral for a unique person'. It was a brilliant gesture and made William a much more satisfied young man. Now, officially, the stuffy protocol that his mother had fought against all her adult life could be thrown out of the window and the ideas of the 'family committee' could prevail. It was a remarkable breakthrough.

At one of the subsequent committee meetings, William read out a newspaper report which emphasised that old protocol reserved state funerals for monarchs or top-rank generals, winners of wars, but because Diana was none of these, she should be granted a lower-rank funeral. New protocol would not permit that. But the people showed they loved her, that she was royalty's superstar, the people's princess, so new protocol demanded a unique funeral for her. Old protocol said the funeral procession was a matter for the palace courtiers; new protocol said that the people's princess should be seen by all those who wanted to pay their respects to her cortège. Old protocol said a monarch was not required to offer a public tribute to the deceased; new protocol said she should be publicly harangued in the press until she did. Old protocol made no provision for a pop star to sing at such a funeral; new protocol invited Elton John.

*Right: With Eton
friends at the Guard's
polo, June 1997.*

*Opposite page:
Vancouver, Canada,
March 1998.*

What occurred in Britain in that extraordinary, memorable week was unprecedented in the history of the monarchy. Protocol and tradition, rejected and resented by Diana, was turned on its head. And one of the people responsible was none other than her own son, William, who was then only fifteen years of age. The British nation, however, had no idea that young William had played a role in such a monumental change of practice in royal traditions which, until then, had been dictated by faceless, grey men whose lives were ruled by historical precedent. The people, the monarch's subjects who shop in the supermarkets, go to football matches, drink in pubs, play bingo and the National Lottery and are addicted to television soaps had made their voices felt and changed the status of protocol. They had no idea that in young William's heart beat the same disdain for empty pomp and ceremony as that which drove his mother for so many years. Now he was carrying the banner, taking over where his mother had left off.

William, accompanied by Harry, had his wish fulfilled on the day before his mother's funeral when he was permitted to walk among the mourners in London, to chat to them, to say 'thank you' to a handful of the people who had massed to say their personal farewells to Diana. Charles, Tiggy Legge-Bourke and his sons had flown from Aberdeen to RAF Northolt in West London earlier that day and had gone to the boys' old home, Kensington Palace, where they used to stay with their mother during school holidays. William and Harry wandered around the apartment, collecting their personal items, some clothes they had always kept there and books and photographs. School uniforms and other items that they would need for the new school term had already been packed and sent to Highgrove. In the drawing room where Diana spent most of her time, the room was still full of the photographs she had framed, nearly all pictures of William and Harry covering the full span of their lives. The photographs covered one wall as well as two tables, all Diana's favourite pictures, demonstrating that Diana did indeed attach great importance to the job of motherhood, as well as showing her harshest critics the love she bore her two boys. William also looked into his mother's old suite of rooms, but only for a moment for the memories were too raw, too unsettling for him to remain there for too long. And there was a public engagement to face.

Dressed in suits and wearing black ties, William and Harry, accompanied by their father, walked out unannounced from Kensington Palace, through the gates that had become a shrine to Diana. The crowds bringing flowers, reading the messages of condolence, checking the gifts left on the palace gates, were taken by surprise seeing Prince Charles, William and Harry walk casually towards them, to talk to those who had come to mourn. Their appearance mesmerised the waiting crowds as well as the hard-nosed cameramen, photographers and journalists who were waiting outside. William, in particular, looked remarkably at ease, the handsome young teenager, tall for his age, an imposing figure, keen to meet and chat and shake the hands of the throng of people standing behind the barriers. To everyone, Wills and Harry just kept repeating 'Thank you, thank you' over and over again. But they were not saying 'Thank you' for the gifts of flowers pressed into their hands, but on behalf of their mother to whom the visitors had come to pay their respects and show their love. At first, the boys seemed taken aback by the sheer volume of floral tributes in front of the black and gold iron gates, but they relaxed as soon as they began talking to those who wanted to shake their hands and give them tokens of respect. Over and over, as William and Harry spoke or listened to the well-wishers, the princes offered their gratitude for the shared sense of loss. They grasped as many outstretched hands as they could, accepted as many flowers as they could carry and thanked everyone they met. People in the crowd wept openly at the sight of the two boys, now left without a mother. And yet both William and Harry behaved with a maturity, Diana would have been proud, even blushing at unforced applause from the onlookers who were surprised by the remarkably relaxed demeanour of the two boys. At times, numbers of people shouted 'We love you' and 'God bless you' and William and Harry waved as a mark of appreciation for the kind sentiments. Then it was time to go and a royal car arrived to whisk them away to St James's Palace, Charles's London home, where they would be staying the night before the funeral. Onlookers down the Mall saw the royal car and the two boys inside and, as the car swept slowly by, the crowds cheered and applauded. In their hands, William and Harry held a single white lily, the traditional symbol of death.

The following morning, William woke early and immediately turned on the television to see what was happening on the streets of London where, in a few hours, the cortège bearing his mother's body would slowly wind its way from Kensington Palace to Westminster Abbey. William saw pictures of the tens of thousands of people who had braved the September cold to camp out overnight, determined to get a good vantage point from which they could witness Diana's final journey. William saw men, women and even children who had camped out that night, struggling out of their sleeping bags in the cool, early morning mist that hung over the capital. Shortly after dawn, those who had kept vigil were joined by hundreds of thousands who had left their homes in the early hours to secure a good position from which to watch the day's events. There were no dark suits and black ties along the route, not because the mourners had no respect for Diana but because, in her life, she had dressed like them on so many occasions; in shorts, a sweat shirt, a baseball cap and trainers, showing a healthy disregard for the formality and the stuffiness of royal protocol. But William would dress for his mother's funeral in a dark lounge suit, black tie and white shirt, for that was expected of him. This was not an occaision for the informality their mother had advocated through most of her life.

Prince Charles saw the boys at breakfast and asked if they wanted to join him, Earl Spencer and Prince Philip in walking immediately behind the gun carriage that would bear their mother's body. They would walk the mile from St James's Palace along the Mall, through Horse Guards Parade and down Whitehall to Westminster Abbey. William answered his father immediately saying that he and Harry had discussed the idea and very much wanted to be a part of the funeral. After breakfast, they dressed in their suits and black ties and continued to watch the spectacle on television. To accommodate the million or more people who wanted to line the route, it had been decided that instead of leaving from St James's Palace, as originally planned, the cortège would start a further mile away at Kensington Palace, Diana's home for most of her adult life. William and Harry sat spellbound that morning as they watched the pictures, showing the antique gun carriage drawn by six black horses and accompanied by nine members of the King's Troop, Royal Horse Artillery, and flanked by a bearer-party of twelve Welsh Guardsmen of the Prince of Wales's Company. But William was watching the reaction of the crowds, many in tears, some throwing white flowers over the coffin which was draped in a Royal Standard. There were cries of 'God bless you' and 'We love you' but, for the most part there was a tense silence, broken only by the sound of people openly grieving. Many hugged each other for comfort, desperate to be consoled; others gripped handkerchiefs and tissues and stood holding them to their faces, alternately wiping away their tears and choking back the emotion that overwhelmed them.

William, Harry, Charles, Earl Spencer and Prince Philip gathered in St James's Palace, waiting for the moment when they would leave the protection of the historic building and walk out into the autumn sunshine to take their place behind the cortège. The television cameras focused on the five men – three generations of royalty – as they stood in silence waiting for the carriage to pass by them en route to the Abbey. William and Harry had been advised to keep their heads down, to look at the ground in front of them – for, in that way, they would not succumb so easily to the pressure and the atmosphere of grief and sorrow all around them. Each step William and Harry took during that mile long walk was watched by the massed ranks of mourners lining the streets. The silence was almost eerie for the two boys except for the muffled sound of the horses' hooves pulling the gun carriage – all William and Harry could hear was the quiet sobbing and weeping of the onlookers along the route. But, somehow, their strength survived the extraordinary ordeal and they managed to make the Abbey without breaking down.

'William and Harry, we all care desperately for you today ... How great your suffering is, we can not even imagine.'

Later, William would confess that the funeral service was almost a blur, save for two memorable events; one was the extraordinary, courageous tribute that Earl Spencer made to his sister, and the other was Elton John's rendition of 'Candle In The Wind', the words of which he had amended to read 'Goodbye, England's rose'. Indeed, the only time that William appeared to be fighting the tears welling up in his eyes was during Earl Spencer's tribute in which he pledged, in Diana's memory, to protect her two 'beloved sons' from the anguish and tearful despair caused by the paparazzi. 'William and Harry', Earl Spencer said, addressing them personally from the pulpit, 'we all care desperately for you today. We are all chewed up with the sadness at the loss of a woman who was not even our mother. How great your suffering is, we cannot even imagine.'

William looked up during the last few paragraphs of his uncle's tribute watching anxiously to see whether Earl Spencer would break down, torn apart by the emotion he felt for Diana. William could tell that Earl Spencer's voice kept breaking, that he was struggling to complete his speech, the words sticking in his throat as he fought to stop the tears. And William looked around the Abbey when he heard the cheers and applause outside in the streets at the end of the hard-hitting tribute, the applause reaching a remarkable crescendo as hundreds of thousands of people gave their support to Earl Spencer's promise to continue 'the imaginative and loving way in which you were steering these two exceptional young men, so that their souls are not simply immersed by duty and tradition but can sing openly as you planned.' And William shared a look with Harry as the two thousand people in the Abbey, five hundred of them representatives of Diana's favourite charities, took up the cheers and began applauding. William knew that no one ever applauds at funerals, especially funerals of such magnitude, and he looked confused when he realised the cheers had even been taken up by those privileged to be in the cloistered confines of the abbey, for they had found it impossible to ignore the common urge to applaud. Not sure whether he, too, should join in, William, followed by Harry, finally decided that he wanted to and a smile crept across his face as he found himself eagerly clapping his uncle's tribute, not caring if he was breaking the strict rules of protocol or not.

After Diana's coffin had been borne from the Abbey to the hearse outside, the Royal Family trooped out to a fleet of waiting cars. Some cars took the Queen, Prince Philip and other members of the Royal Family to Northolt for their flight back to Aberdeen and the seclusion of Balmoral Castle. But Prince Charles, Earl Spencer, Diana's sisters Jane and Sarah and Diana's mother, Mrs Frances Shand Kydd, along with William and Harry, took their cars to the railway station for the journey to Althorp, the Spencer family home in Northamptonshire, where Diana had grown up. Television cameras were banned for the private burial service on an island in the middle of an oval lake in the grounds of Althorp House. William and Harry stood beside the grave with other members of Diana's family waiting for the cortège, which had been delayed by more an an hour due to the crowds that flanked the path of the hearse and it's police escort throughout the eighty mile journey from London. The vicar from the local church and six pallbearers accompanied the coffin from the hearse to the grave and the two boys watched as it was slowly lowered into the grave. Prayers were said, holy water was sprinkled on the coffin and, within ten minutes, the ceremony was over. Wills and Harry saw their mother laid to rest and the two lads walked with their father and uncle to Althorp House for tea and sandwiches. An hour later, the two boys, accompanied by their father, drove to Highgrove in Gloucestershire where they arrived in time for dinner.

Opposite top: Prince William, June 1997.

Opposite below: William takes a nasty fall during a rugby game at Eton, March 1996.

A smile crept across his face as he found himself eagerly clapping his uncle's tribute, not caring if he was breaking the strict rules of protocol or not.

Their rooms had been prepared, their clothes had been sent from London to Highgrove, but neither William nor Harry were ready to go to bed. The longest day in their young lives had seemed to contain so much emotion that they wanted to savour the memories, to think of everything that had occurred that day; the weeping mourners, their mother's cortège, the service in the abbey and the final moments when they saw their mother laid to rest in her grave at Althorp. But shortly after 10.30 that evening, persuaded by their father, they did finally go to their beds.

Sunday, September 7, dawned bright and sunny and Charles decided that his sons should get out and about rather than staying at home with their memories. Tiggy Legge-Bourke had also travelled to Highgrove and she and Charles determined, without fuss or haste, to encourage Wills and Harry to look to the future, to the forthcoming school year, to their sporting activities and to meeting their friends back at boarding school. Though both boys should have started the new term later that week, it was decided they would stay at Highgrove with Charles and Tiggy, relaxing and getting used to a new life, one without their beloved mother. Those few days went well and both William and Harry enjoyed the outdoors with Tiggy and their father. They would go for walks together, go horse riding and swimming and Tiggy would play football with them in the garden. Charles asked the cook to give the boys their favourite foods, to spoil them in any way they wanted, to make them feel they were precious and wanted and loved.

William had been behaving more like a parent towards Harry than an older brother.

Charles made sure his sons were never alone during those days of coming to terms with their mother's death and everything that had happened. He involved them in everything, encouraged them to get out and do whatever they wanted and spent most of the time with them. If he wasn't around, then Tiggy would always be present, not permitting them to feel lonely or unloved. William, in particular, sought the presence of his father during those five days. It was as though he felt lost and needed someone to lean on as a support, as a haven of safety, of protection, someone who had the power to guard against all the evils of the world, and especially against the horror of death. William would talk to his father about the car crash, asking him questions which had not been satisfactorily answered by the television pundits nor by the newspapers which still wrote daily of the facts they were unearthing surrounding the details of the accident. William wanted to know who should take the blame for the death of his mother, though he continued to lay most of the blame on the tabloid press and the scavenging photographers.

Before the following weekend, both boys said they were fully prepared to return to their respective schools, William to Eton and Harry to Ludgrove. For William, however, there was also a feeling of guilt, a twinge of conscience that he was leaving Harry to fight his own corner when William knew that his mother had always asked him to protect Harry. Ever since the car crash, William had been behaving more like a parent towards Harry rather than an older brother, in keeping with what he believed his mother would have wanted and thoroughly approved of. Indeed, ever since William and Harry had been told of the death of their mother, William had been at pains hardly ever to let Harry out of his sight. William spoke to his father, and to Tiggy, about this predicament and sense of guilt and they both assured him that, once back at school,

Harry would be fine. They also assured him that if Harry needed to phone William, then the headmaster would understand and allow him to do so at any time. For Harry, it would be his final year at Ludgrove before he, too, would join his brother at Eton in September 1998. Both William and Harry were, reportedly, happy to back at school, their daily lives full with lessons, activities, sports events and the rough and tumble of boarding school life, helping them to get over the tragedy that had struck so hard and so swiftly. William, in particular, enjoyed being back with his close friends, all of whom had been told that, after offering their condolences to William over the death of his mother, to refrain from discussing or mentioning the matter. And, as before, the daily newspapers were first scrutinised by a master before being handed to William, with any offending or offensive articles about his mother or father being removed. In fact, the daily chore was futile because William could see any newspaper he wanted, any day he wished, simply by going into Windsor and buying one. However, no matter how tempted he may have been, it is understood that he never did, mainly because his mother had always warned him against what the papers wrote about the Royal Family for, she believed, the tabloids usually wrote inaccurate, offensive rubbish which had no bearing on the true facts.

William was relieved to be back in the protective atmosphere of Eton among his friends. He loved the anonymity of Eton life where no one paid him any special attention; where he could chat and relax and have fun with his pals like any other Eton boy. It was all so very different from the overbearing glare of the spotlight that he had faced during the funeral. And William loathes the public limelight, hates being the centre of attention, for it always forcefully reminds him of the treatment his mother suffered at the hands of the photographers and the tabloid press.

Diana had tried to persuade William that the cameras and press attention were a necessary evil.

Indeed, William came through the ordeal of his mother's death and highly public funeral with flying colours, surprising everyone who knew of his natural enmity towards the press and personal publicity. In her life, Diana had tried to persuade William that the cameras and press attention were a necessary evil and that he had learn to live with them. William knew that his mother would have expected him to behave with maturity and equanimity towards the cameras on this most public occasion, and that was probably one of the reasons he surprised everyone with his calmness, sense of responsibility and his acceptance of routine traditional duty.

Christmas, 1997, was of course a very difficult, if not traumatic, time for both William and Harry and, indeed, for the entire Royal Family. The family all realised that they had to handle the festive season in a delicate, unobtrusive way, making sure they did not ignore the fact that Diana was no longer around but also trying to make sure William and Harry enjoyed themselves, never allowing them to lapse into sentimental feelings of loneliness and grief which would only hinder their efforts to come to terms with their mother's death. For most of the time, Charles, aided by Tiggy and their 19-year-old cousin Peter Phillips, did, for the most part, manage to make Sandringham a laughter-filled, happy, environment for Wills and Harry. But their mother was not forgotten.

When they all went to church on Christmas day, prayers were offered for the repose of the soul of Diana, Princess of Wales, and William was happy that his mother had been publicly remembered. Christmas, naturally was a hard time for William and he missed his mother terribly but, despite the feeling of loss, he put on a brave face, mainly for the sake of Harry, who seemed to be racing around Sandringham, enjoying himself immensely. Throughout the Christmas holiday, however, William could never forget those last few Christmases following the official separation of his parents. Those times had been tough for him. He knew that Diana had been staying on her own in London while he and Harry accompanied their father to Sandringham for the Royal Family's traditional Christmas gathering. William recalled that those Christmases at Sandringham had not been fun, in fact the very opposite. He remembered the times he had talked to his mother on the phone and how sad he had felt, hearing her unhappiness on the phone, knowing that she was missing him and Harry so much that she was near to tears. He recalled the times that he tried to be brave, keeping a stiff upper lip, but had often cried himself to sleep at night in the solitude and secrecy of his bed. William knew that no one had realised how awful those days had been for him; for most of the time he only wanted to be with his mother, hoping that she was OK, that she wasn't too sad at being parted from her sons. Those days also made him feel isolated and helpless because he could do nothing to rectify the situation. He understood that his father and other members of the Royal Family tried to make amends, to create a happy, fun-filled Christmas atmosphere for him and Harry, as well as the other young royals who came to stay. But he had found it difficult to laugh, to enjoy himself or to join in the enthusiastic games and Christmas festivities.

As a result, William was more than happy to return to the friendly atmosphere of Eton, to be among his friends once again where he could relax and concentrate on school work, games and enjoying school life. But Christmas 1997 had been by far the worst time of all. It wasn't that the Royal Family had been anything but kind, considerate and understanding throughout the holidays; it was simply the fact that being with them reminded him every waking moment of the death of his beloved mother; and every time he thought of her, tears came to his eyes.

For six months following Diana's funeral, William never made a public appearance and, as a result of the battering the tabloids were given by the British people following Diana's death, no photographs and very few newspaper articles were written about either William or Harry. The newspapers had finally backed off, giving the young princes the peace which they needed to come to terms with their mother's death. William knew in his heart that the tabloids and the paparazzi had left them alone because they felt partly responsible for Diana's death. In his tribute to Diana, Earl Spencer said, 'There is no doubt that she was looking for a new direction in her life at the time of her death. She talked endlessly of getting away from England, mainly because of the treatment that she received at the hands of the newspapers. I don't think she ever understood why her genuinely good intentions were sneered at by the media, why there appeared to be a permanent quest on their behalf to bring her down.'

William had not realised that his mother had contemplated moving abroad, leaving him and Harry behind, but he did understand the appaling, disgraceful pressure she was put under every time she appeared in public. William understood that Diana could not travel anywhere in Britain, whether to the shops, the gym, the cinema or out to dinner, without half-a-dozen paparazzi dogging her every step and snapping away with their cameras, sometimes making it difficult for her to walk down a street as they poked their cameras within feet of her face, determined to get as close as possible to their victim. In fact, Diana was not considering leaving Wills and Harry behind. She was searching for a home where she could live in peace and comfort, somewhere abroad, a place hidden from the public gaze or the prying lenses of cameramen, where she could escape to during term times when Wills and Harry were away at school and, more importantly, a home where Wills and Harry could stay happily with her during their school holidays.

Earl Spencer's attacks on the British tabloids received unequivocal support from the vast majority of the British people, and the tabloid proprietors and editors knew that if they hounded and pestered Diana's young sons in the way they had hounded their mother, the British public would react with anger and the newspapers would suffer, they would be hit where it hurt, in their pockets. As a result, the Press Complaints Commission, the body charged with enforcing the Code of Practice for editors to follow, met in urgent session after Diana's death, to consider what new measures should be implemented. Journalists, photographers, cameramen and anyone associated with the media had been given a rough ride by the public – 'scum' was the word often heard during those days following Diana's death, a sentiment with which William agreed with entirely.

Three weeks after the funeral, Lord Wakeham, Chairman of the Press Complaints Commission, issued a statement in which he outlined a new, stricter code for the media to follow. He dealt with harrassment of individuals, especially celebrities and members of the Royal Family; he proposed that the industry should prohibit the publication of pictures obtained through 'persistent pursuit or as a result of unlawful behaviour. And he tried to control the practice of freelance paparazzi photographers used by newspapers to obtain 'exclusive' pictures, demanding the picture agencies employing the paparazzi sign up to the Code of Practice. And in a bid to protect William and Harry, as well as other children of famous parents, Lord Wakeham said newspapers could have no excuse for invading the privacy of a child because newspapers should recognise the particularly vulnerable position of children whose parents are in the public eye.

The young, somewhat shy, modest boy the world had known, had matured into a confident, remarkably handsome and tall young man with a winning smile.

As a result, newspapers, television cameramen and even the great majority of freelance paparazzi photographers kept away from William and Harry following Diana's death, not daring to risk the anger of readers and viewers in a bid to win back the respect of the nation. More importantly, the newspaper proprietors and chairmen of television companies gave orders to their editors to leave the young princes alone. However, one or two paparazzi did tail William and his pals when they ventured from Eton into Windsor to go shopping or have tea in the town. Some photographers took long lens shots of William rowing on the Thames but though these pictures were offered to Britain's tabloid editors none of them bought or published the shots.

But young William was growing up, fast. The first sign that William was becoming a cult figure, perhaps even an object of desire among the teenagers, was in November, 1997, when he attended a lunch at the Royal Naval College in Greenwich, celebrating his grandparents' 50th wedding anniversary. Six hundred screaming teenage girls heralded his arrival, much to the surprise of everyone else attending the lunch. No one had seen such a reaction to the youthful William's appearance and even the police were taken aback for no one was expecting such a screaming reception. In fact, the first signs that Prince William might become a pin-up occurred two years earlier, in October, 1995, when *Smash Hits* published a poster of a boyish William dressed in uncool blazer, tie and grey trousers. It was a sell-out. Five months later, William received 54 Valentine cards; a year later he had more than 500. In 1998, he received more than 1,000!

But the photographs of William taken during his visit to Canada in March, 1998, still came as a great surprise to the British people. The young, somewhat shy, modest boy the world had known, had matured into a confident, remarkably handsome and tall young man with a winning smile. Everyone who saw the television pictures, as well as those published in newspapers across the world, immediately drew a comparison with his mother. In Diana's first pictures she, too, had appeared shy, modest, and even timid. And what threw many people who saw the handsome William was the likeness between Diana and William. Today, William bears a haunting resemblance to his mother, with her engaging smile and fair hair. In fact, William closely resembles his late grandfather, the former Earl Spencer, when he was a dashing young army officer, commissioned into the Royal Scots Greys. He became an equerry to both King George VI and to the Queen. In the late 1940s and 1950s, the tall, dashing Johnny Spencer was considered one of the most handsome young men in London, and invited to all the most elegant social events.

During his 1998 visit to Canada with his father and young Harry, William was exposed to the full treatment – the adulation of screaming, teenage girls. He was totally taken aback by the reception the Vancouver girls gave him, screaming at him 'I love you' whenever he appeared in public. At first, he did not know how to react to such enthusiastic excitement. When he arrived at Vancouver's Waterfront Centre Hotel on the first evening of the holiday, he looked nervously towards the group of two hundred teenage girls screaming for his attention, put his head down and walked briskly into the hotel, disappointing his fans. But his father, who had witnessed William's arrival, knew that he had to persuade young William to cope with such scenes, for he knew that this would be only the first of many, perhaps hundreds or thousands, of such scenes over the coming years. Prince Charles knew that William and Harry would have to face a far sterner test than he ever had to endure in his youth. But William had touched a chord in the hearts of Vancouver's female set for he is unique. He is not only a royal prince, heir to the British throne, but he is also a handsome, good-looking young man, and the son of Princess Diana who became an icon throughout the world.

That evening in Vancouver, Charles talked to William, explaining that this was his first great test following his remarkably mature presence at the time of his mother's death. Charles

'He's rich, he's gorgeous and he's a prince. What more do you need?'

explained that being a royal prince, a member of the House of Windsor and heir to the British throne, meant that appearing in public was one of the duties he would have to face and get used to. Charles understood that William hated the press and, in particular, the paparazzi and the tabloid photographers, but explained that he and Harry would have to learn to live with photographers because they would be a part of his life, for ever. The following morning, Charles, William and Harry made a private visit to the Pacific Space Centre in Vancouver, but somehow the young girls had learned of the visit and two hundred waited to see their Prince Charming. As the visit was private, the girls only managed to catch a fleeting glimpse of their new idol but the screams of hysteria could be heard throughout the building.

William would be greeted by even more abundant adulation and louder screams when he visited Burnaby South Secondary School in Vancouver. The manic screaming was like nothing William had ever faced before, when three hundred teenage girls, tears streaming down their cheeks, appeared desperate to shake William's hand or simply to touch him. 'William, William, William,' they screamed at the young prince, who walked towards them, smiling broadly, as though he had enjoyed such experiences many times before. But William was learning fast. In a matter of days, he had learned to cope with the screaming adulation and act as if such receptions were an everyday event. This time he stood his ground, smiled like a professional and seemed in command of the situation, happily shaking the hands of his adolescent admirers, accepting their gifts of cuddly toys, dodging the daffodils the girls threw towards him, and pressing the flesh like a Hollywood star. The screams, the tears, the anguished hormonal wailing, reminiscent of the adulation showered on pop icons, had been a revelation to him. And yet, in the matter of a few hours, William had learned how to cope with such strident acclamation. When a group of girls were asked why they found William so appealing, attractive and desirable, one answered, 'He's rich, he's gorgeous and he's a prince. What more do you need?'

But the *pièce de résistance* came during the last official stop of the visit at the heritage centre on the Vancouver waterfront. The main feature was supposed to be a speech by Prince Charles, but the five hundred girls who turned up had other ideas. Struggling for breath between sobs and screams, the girls offered William flowers, teddy bears, tear-stained handkerchiefs and eternal love. William strolled from side to side, smiling, shaking hands and saying 'thank you' to one and all in exactly the same way as his mother had done a thousand times during her lifetime. And, on this occasion, Wills even behaved like his mother, looking slightly bashful, ill-at-ease and shy, just as any teenager would have done, when faced with such unbridled teenage passion. Then, unexpectedly and dramatically, Wills totally stole the occasion. After accepting a gift of a baseball jacket and 'poor boy' cap, Wills shook off his own jacket and slipped into his new clothes – cap peak at the back of course – and then twirled and gave a rap-style roll of wrist and shoulders. His bit of fun had been spontaneous; no one in the royal party was aware William was planning any such gesture. Indeed, due to his natural antipathy towards the cameras, the photographers and television crews were also taken aback. The audience, however, was delirious, the crescendo of cheering adoration almost deafening.

Opposite Page: Princess Diana's coffin arriving at Westminster Abbey.

In that gesture, Prince William seemed to enjoy the limelight for the first time. He also seemed blissfully unaware of the cameras and the photographers who clicked away madly as they scrambled to get pictures of the world's newest superstar. 'Willsmania' had arrived. Prince Harry was not forgotten either in the mayhem. Though Harry was only thirteen, a number of the girls wanted to shake his hand and touch him, but not with the same raw passion as they showed towards his elder brother. Indeed, Harry thoroughly enjoyed the occasion, goading his elder brother into moving from one group of admirers to another so he could see the hysterical reaction that was generated. Harry was laughing at the responses the girls showed to his brother's presence, urging William to continue his new-found role as the great attraction of the Royal House of Windsor. For his part, Prince Charles looked on with admiration, fully realising that here, indeed, the Royal Family had a new star who commanded such adulation. But Charles, who had also been the centre of media attention during his early years, realised that he would have to ration William's appearances wherever they went to enable his son to concentrate on his education, his exams and his future role. The extraordinary scenes, however, did much to liven up the royal visit to Canada which was really meant to be a private skiing holiday for the three of them rather than a baptism of fire for William. For the greater part of this trip, cameramen and photographers did leave the royal party in peace, happily cutting a deal for a photo-opportunity on the ski slopes before agreeing to leave them entirely alone to enjoy their holiday. But, on one occasion, when Charles, William and Harry walked into a mountain café for a bite to eat, the three hundred skiers enjoying their lunch rose to their feet as one and applauded the royal party. That standing ovation was entirely spontaneous, a sign of the warmth Canadians feel towards the British Royal Family, and the moment cheered Charles.

The holiday was a tonic for Charles and his sons and getting away from Britain for a week to enjoy the sun and the snow helped to forge a closer bond between the three of them. It was the first time Wills and Harry had been alone with their father since the traumatic days following their mother's death; but this was a holiday together and the three of them appeared to be very much at ease with each other, as though they had discovered a new, binding relationship. No longer would Wills and Harry have to juggle their affections towards one or other of their parents; no longer would they be forced to make choices as to whether they wanted to spend weekends or holidays with their father or their mother; no longer would they feel compelled to take sides, supporting one against the other; and no longer would there be atmospheres fraught with friction as the boys floated between their parents' homes.

His upper-body strength and athletic physique has propelled William into Britain's top one hundred swimmers for his age.

And William, in particular, has now found a new role model, his own father, who can understand more than anyone the strains and pressures of being an heir to the throne; who knows the problems that hero-worship will bring to his son; and who also knows that the British press has a nasty way of building up the nation's heroes only to revel in knocking them down at a later stage. Charles will do his utmost to protect his sons as best he can, but he now knows that he has the duty of advising and guiding a superstar.

He also knows that William will find it far easier thwarting the lustful desires of young fourteen- and fifteen-year-olds than the twenty-somethings who will soon find the handsome, good-looking young William irresistible, a target for their more focused demands and amorous ambitions.

William will take his A-levels at Eton and, if successful, he is expected to go to Oxford or Cambridge. Prince Charles went to Cambridge but Diana's brother, Charles, went to Magdalen College, Oxford. It is expected that the final decision will be taken at the time on the advice of those Eton masters who have had responsibility for William's education. After university, William is likely to spend some time in one of the services; Army, Royal Navy or Royal Air Force. He might, however, like his father, learn to fly with the RAF and then move to the Royal Navy. Only time will tell.

The question that every teenage girl now wants answered is exactly what kind of young man William is. What's he *really* like. Well, many are surprised when they meet him. At first he is shy and bashful, self-effacing and sometimes awkward. But that is only a protective shell behind which he hides whenever he meets new people or a fresh situation. He has every reason to be guarded for he trusts no one. He knows that many will tell tales about him, sell stories to the tabloids and, if necessary, sell him down the river. So, William puts up his guard and only slowly permits people to become close to him. He will surreptitiously watch strangers who have entered his circle, trying to calculate whether he should trust them or blank them. It is a problem that few sixteen-year-olds have to think about, but to William it is incredibly important. As a result, young William has had to mature faster than the average teenager and those adults who meet and chat to him describe him as two or three years older than his actual age.

But in his three years at Eton, William has forged close relationships with half-a-dozen boys of his own age. He gets on well with them and they, in turn, treat him no differently from other boys at the school. He loves that. He is known for his sense of fun, his engaging smile, his relaxed attitude and his determination to succeed, whether at sport or academically. William has fitted in very well at Eton and has thrived in the culture of the school, which has a reputation of being able to absorb all kinds of boys from different backgrounds and encourage them to become confident, outgoing young men who know they are a breed apart. The school also encourages all the boys to work hard and pushes them to excel in whatever area they choose, whether it is languages, classics, science or sport. William, it seems, is enjoying not only the camaraderie and anonymity of Eton, but also the academic and sporting challenges the school has to offer.

Since the death of his mother, William has become far more confident and sure of himself. And Eton has helped the young man to relax and enjoy himself far more than when he first arrived at the school, when he was a shy, introvert and wary teenager, unsure of himself and his capabilities. At first, he felt that the other boys at Eton were more intelligent than him and he worked hard to prove himself. Academically, William has done well and is certainly one of the most conscientious boys in his class. As a result, every exam he has sat, including three O-levels, he has passed with ease. This summer he is due to sit a further six O-levels and was tipped to pass all of these as well. He has already proved that he certainly has brains. And he uses them.

William also has brawn. At first, William enjoyed rowing at Eton and in the summer term of 1997 he could be seen frequently sculling on the Thames. Such exercise builds great arm, back and leg muscles and with his natural development, William blossomed into a powerful young man for his age. During the summer of 1997, however, he had been persuaded to switch to swimming, his mother's favourite sport, and he has proved an exceptional talent. His upper-body strength and athletic physique has propelled William into Britain's top one hundred swimmers for his age in the 50-metre freestyle. In March, 1998, he won Eton's junior 100-metre and 50-metre freestyle and clocked the fastest time since 1987 at the Berkshire County schools finals. The current fastest 50 metres for a British 15-year-old is 24.95 seconds, only three seconds under William's best time. If William decided to train with a professional coach, Britain's Amateur Swimming Association spopkesmen believe the heir to the throne could become a serious challenger for national honours. But that would involve strict and tough practice schedules, and swimming at least twice a day, every day, with his own personal trainer. It may be that William would like to accept that challenge, following in the footsteps of his aunt, Princess Anne, who represented Britain in three-day eventing in the Olympics, as well as his hero, Peter Phillips, who played rugby for Scotland.

William is already a natural athlete. He enjoys a number of sports, including rowing, football and water polo. He has played rugby but doesn't enjoy that winter sport as much as football, in which he has shown real talent. William also plays tennis and squash, two sports where he has shown quite exceptional talent, his tall, powerful physique giving him an advantage over boys of his own age. He is also a competent skier and has become quite a daredevil on the slopes, now outpacing his father on some of the most difficult off-piste slopes at Klosters in Switzerland, Aspen, in Colorado, USA, and in Canada. He loves the challenge of racing downhill. And, of course, there are the country pursuits which he enjoys with his father and Tiggy. In all these he has revealed a keen interest and real competence. He is now a better shot than Tiggy and she was always considered very competent. One of the reasons William has proved such a natural talent at most sports is because of the competitive side of his nature which belies the image he portrays in public. People simply do not realise how determined, earnest and resolute William can be when playing sports. He likes to win. He believes that he must prove himself more than any other contemporary, simply because of his position, the son of the Prince of Wales. He asks for no quarter and gives none in any sport. He also reveals a stubborness, refusing to be beaten, never giving up even when the situation looks hopeless. In the team games William plays, he shows a great capacity for encouraging others, one of the reasons he was made captain of Ludgrove's first football XI. He is seen as a natural leader.

William has been born into royalty, trained to understand his role and the part he will play.

In the privacy of his room at Eton, as well as his bedroom at home, Wills loves to shut himself away and listen to rock music, so very different from the classical and opera music which his father prefers. William will often walk around with his Walkman listening to loud, hard rock music, oblivious to everyone around him. The British band *Pulp* is one his great favourites. He has also been smitten by the *Spice Girls*, and loves their raunchy style. And he knows how to dress. In the American *People* magazine's 'Best Dressed People of 1996' the editors wrote, 'He looks and dresses

like a model. He makes no mistakes.' And William's dress sense covers every facet of his life, whether he is dressing in classical English tweeds and brogues like his father, designer T-shirts, jeans and sneakers when wearing casual apparel or dressing with style and colour when skiing. Of course, William enjoyed his mother's astute guidance for many years. It remains to be seen whether he will now develop his own inimitable style, coupled with good taste and a knack of always looking good in whatever he wears.

Engulfed in cheering crowds, Vancouver, Canada, March 1998.

The question that young ladies around the world, and a number of mothers, will soon be debating is which young woman Prince William will one day marry. Most people believe that young William has the character, personality and natural gifts of his mother; that in his maturity, he will have the same gentle touch, the same spontaneous reaction to those less fortunate; the same compassion, a symbol of selfless humanity coupled with a sense of duty and a natural nobility. He also has considerable sex appeal. From now on, his public appearances are likely to evoke a voracious public interest, more enthusiastic, more hysterical and more frenzied than those that greeted his mother. In some ways, it does appear that the young are transferring their adoration of Diana to young William; and the people who threw their support behind Diana and her troubled life also seem to want to do all they can to support both William and Harry. But at least William is better prepared to deal with the acclaim than Diana ever was. William has been born into royalty, trained to understand his role and the part he will play. Already, the signs are there that William will indeed develop into the person Diana had been guiding him towards – a people's prince.

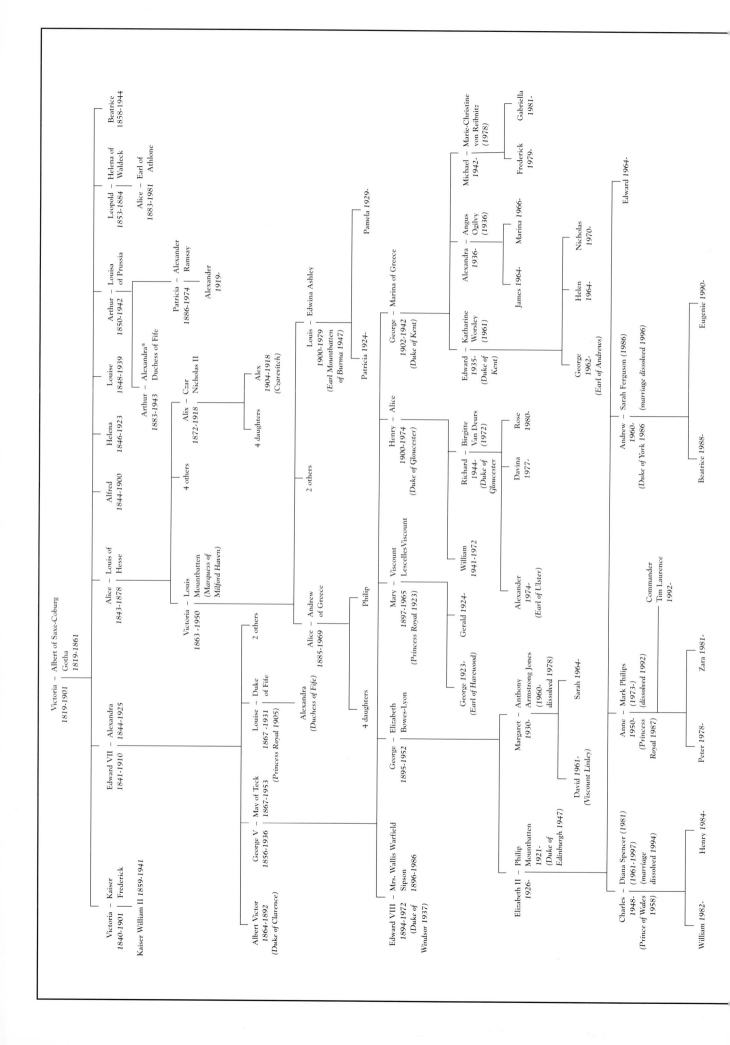

Victoria – Albert of Saxe-Coburg
1819-1901   Gotha
               1819-1861

Victoria – Kaiser
1840-1901   Frederick

Kaiser William II 1859-1941

Edward VII – Alexandra
1841-1910   1844-1925

Alice – Louis of
1843-1878   Hesse

Alfred
1844-1900

Helena
1846-1923

Louise
1848-1939

Arthur – Louisa
1850-1942   of Prussia

Leopold – Helena of
1853-1884   Waldeck

Beatrice
1858-1944

Arthur – Alexandra*
1883-1943   Duchess of Fife

Alice – Earl of
1883-1981   Athlone

Victoria – Louis
1863-1950   Mountbatten
            (Marquess of
            Milford Haven)

4 others

Alix – Czar
1872-1918 Nicholas II

Alex
1904-1918
(Czareuitch)

4 daughters

Patricia – Alexander
1886-1974   Ramsay

Alexander
1919-

Louis – Edwina Ashley
1900-1979
(Earl Mountbatten
of Burma 1947)

Patricia 1924-

Pamela 1929-

Albert Victor
1864-1892
(Duke of Clarence)

George V – May of Teck
1856-1936   1867-1953

Louise – Duke
1867-1931   of Fife
(Princess Royal 1905)

Alexandra
(Duchess of Fife)

Andrew – Alice
of Greece   1885-1969

Philip

4 daughters

2 others

George – Marina of Greece
1902-1942
(Duke of Kent)

Mary – Viscount
1897-1965   LescellesViscount
(Princess Royal 1923)

George 1923-
(Earl of Harewood)

Gerald 1924-

Henry – Alice
1900-1974
(Duke of Gloucester)

William
1941-1972

Richard – Birgitte
1944-   Van Deurs
(Duke of   (1972)
Gloucester)

Alexander
1974-
(Earl of Ulster)

Davina
1977-

Rose
1980-

Edward – Katharine
1935-   Worsley
(Duke of   (1961)
Kent)

Alexandra – Angus
1936-   Ogilvy
           (1936)

Michael – Marie-Christine
1942-   von Reibnitz
          (1978)

George
1962-
(Earl of Andrews)

Helen
1964-

James 1964-

Marina 1966-

Nicholas
1970-

Frederick
1979-

Gabriella
1981-

Edward VIII – Mrs. Wallis Warfield
1894-1972   Sipson
(Duke of   1896-1986
Windsor 1937)

Elizabeth II – Philip
1926-   Mountbatten
             1921-
             (Duke of
             Edinburgh 1947)

George – Elizabeth
1895-1952   Bowes-Lyon

Margaret – Anthony
1930-   Armstrong Jones
           (1960-
           dissolved 1978)

David 1961-
(Viscount Linley)

Sarah 1964-

Charles – Diana Spencer (1981)
1948-   (1961-1997)
(Prince of   (marriage
Wales   dissolved 1994)
1958)

William 1982-

Henry 1984-

Anne – Mark Philips
1950-   (1973-)
(Princess   (dissolved 1992)
Royal 1987)

Commander
Tim Laurence
1992-

Peter 1978-

Zara 1981-

Andrew – Sarah Ferguson (1986)
1960-   (marriage dissolved 1996)
(Duke of York 1986)

Edward 1964-

Beatrice 1988-

Eugenie 1990-